WRITING THROUGH THE MESS:
Seeking Healing Through Writing

WRITTEN BY:

ANNE SCHOBER
LISA ROTH WALTER

Published by:
Library Tales Publishing, Inc.
www.LibraryTalesPublishing.com
www.Facebook.com/LibraryTalesPublishing

Copyright © 2017 by Anne Schober
Published by Library Tales Publishing.
New York, New York

For general information on our other products and services, please contact our Customer Care Department at 1-800-754-5016, or fax 917-463-0892. For technical support, please visit www.LibraryTalesPublishing.com

Library Tales Publishing also publishes its books in a variety of electronic formats. Every content that appears in print is available in electronic books.

ISBN-13: 978-0999275849
ISBN-10: 0999275844

PRINTED IN THE UNITED STATES OF AMERICA

This book is dedicated to the writers who will find their voices in the mess, and those who graciously shared their stories with us.

TABLE OF CONTENTS

III. Embracing

A NOTE FROM THE AUTHORS
Why We Believe in the Power of Healing through Writing

<u>Anne</u>

My writing journey began ten years ago when I was asked a profound question: "Who are you? You seem to be so put together, yet there is something hidden behind your smile." I thought about that for a while, smiled, and simply said, "I am what I am." I went home that day and began writing…

I am Virginia Anne Marie Penny Schober. I am a different name to different people, but I am the same person. I am a brunette/blonde/red-haired dyed woman who has no idea what her natural color is, so don't ask. I am the granddaughter of a coal-mining war veteran, a southern elitist, a Yugoslavian immigrant, and a devout Irish Catholic. I am a strong willed, independent, well-mannered and southern at heart woman – a unique combination of my eclectic ancestors.

I am what I am. I am a daughter, a wife, a mother, a teacher, a student, a friend and a dreamer. I am the middle child – the one forgotten in mind but favorite in heart. I am an optimist who believes in the power of positive thinking and the owner of a permanent smile. I am the biggest Notre Dame fan in town – win or lose – so don't even think of messing with my Irish. I am what I am.

I am a transplant from the cotton fields of Alabama to the manure covered farm fields of Pennsylvania. I am a mixture of southern hospitality and northern stinginess. I am older than 18 and younger than 88 – I am the perfect age. I am a parrot-head, Margaritaville, flip-flop, young-at-heart woman with a passion for pink tulips, sunsets and a nice cold glass of….

1

I am what I am. I am shy, outgoing, confident, and uncertain of myself at all times. I am bouncy ball that shoots off in all different directions at any given moment and yet always ends up back where I started. I am a goof! I am what I am. I am respectful of all people, and I expect respect in return. I am imperfect. I make mistakes and like to have them pointed out to me so that I can learn from my own hiccups. I treat others as I expect to be treated. I am fair and honest with a heart as big as the universe.

I am what I am. I am a writer who explores, experiments and dabbles with different genres to tap into my full potential. I am an author and the universe holds my characters. I am a procrastinator, but I know how to get my work done. I accept no lame excuses. I am a writing tutor in the evenings, a passionate public speaker during the day, and a full-time explorer of life. I stand for what I believe in, even when others fall aside. I am a guide, a coach, a friend and a believer. I am what I am.

I placed the pen down, happy with what I had written. The next day, I hand it to the person who challenged me the day before as she looked at me with quizzical eyes, still wondering what was lurking behind my smile.

I began thinking… Why can't I be honest with myself, and others? Why am I scared to share who I really am? There is so much to tell and yet I choose to keep it hidden, afraid that if I dare acknowledge it, if I dare write it down, it will become a reality. But it is there, lurking, waiting. I am what I am. I am a rape victim.

It all began thirty-five years ago…

I was eighteen years old, a college freshman in Erie, PA, far away from friends and family. I was shy. I was lonely. I missed home. I would look out my dorm room window right into the window a prison cell, a piece of glass covered in bars, hiding a prisoner from my sight. Little did I know that I would enter my own prison in a few short weeks.

I remember that night like it was yesterday. I was at a party, wearing jeans, a sweat shirt, my hair pulled back in a ponytail, and bright blue sneakers comfortably carrying me from one beer to the next. As I looked around the darkened basement, I noticed that I was underdressed and I felt completely out of place. I went back for another drink. I tried to find my roommate, but she was lost in the sea of booze, music, and fraternity brothers. I was alone. I went back to the keg and there he was. A senior fraternity member asked if he could pour me another drink. I accepted. He never left my side, making sure my glass was never empty. He asked to dance with me, I said yes. Can you imagine? A freshman grabbing the attention of a senior? Music blared, beer flowed, and he took me upstairs, asking if I would like to have a tour of the house. I was beyond excited. A senior was actually taking interest in me... a freshman who was overweight, underdressed and a mere wallflower.

He grabbed my hand and we walked out of the basement, up the stairs through the kitchen, he grabbing a bottle of booze as we climbed up another flight of stairs, and yet another. "Aren't you going to show me the house?", I asked.

"I am showing you the only room that matters", he responds.

I started to get a bad feeling. We arrived at the very top of the house and into a room that was dark and vacant. He filled my glass with a dark, alcoholic liquid, demanding I drink. I did. He filled it again. Again, I drank. He turned on the stereo. Queens Bohemian Rhapsody blaring. He said I was cute. I wanted to believe him. He said I was someone he dreamed of. I wanted to believe him. The room was swaying and my eyes were getting fuzzy. I was thrown onto a cold and dirty bed. I was screaming. I was hitting. I was kicking. I was scared. No one came. No one heard me. No one rescued me. I heard the words, "Mama, just killed a man...put a gun against his dead, pulled the trigger now he's dead...Momma, didn't mean to make you cry... "coming from the radio and I cried. I screamed. I was being raped. I was being violated. I was helpless. I would never be the same.

He passed out and I grabbed my clothes, shaking and terrified, running from the room, down three flights of stairs into a dark night. Alone. On a vacated street in the middle of Erie. I ran until I could run no more, past the prison and into my dorm. I ran. I ran to the shower, covering myself with soap, hot water and tears. I ran. I ran away from everything that had just happened to me. I ran into my own personal prison. I ran into my own personal hell.

In the weeks that followed, I found myself drinking more, attending class less, and afraid of being out at night. I was drinking fifths of Jack Daniels at a time, engulfing amphetamines and downers, anything to help me escape. I talked to my family less and kept to myself more. I hid from reality, I hid from my pain, I hid from myself.

In late October of my freshman year, I was found passed out on the streets of Erie, floating in a sea of alcohol and pills. I was flown home to be put through a battery of tests to discover "what was wrong with me". All tests came up negative. I knew they would. I was silent. I did not tell anyone what happened to me. It was my secret, my reality, and I could not share it with anyone.

Instead, I went back to my prison, my own personal hell, keeping my secret from everyone. I failed my freshman year, receiving a 0.8 GPA. I was allowed to return to school only if I chose a new major and attend school over the summer. And so, I did. I rented a one bedroom efficiency one block away from the place where my innocence was taken away. I found my comfort and safety in the bottles and drugs that kept me company. I eventually went out on dates, had a boyfriend, met some new friends, but never was myself again. I would never again be the Anne Penny that left my home as a sweet, fun, caring eighteen-year-old. I was now a beaten, scarred, depressed, and different person. more than anyone could imagine. But, I was also a great actress. My family, my friends, no one knew what happened to me because I kept my secret hidden behind my smile. No one could ever know.

Until I met my husband. I had known Mike when we were in high school. He was a year ahead of me, and in the '80's, it was not common to date and/ or like anyone older than yourself. But, he was hot! He would spend a lot of time at my house, partying with my parents, and I quickly became enamored by his humor and, of course, his good looks. He wrote me a letter my sophomore year and when I came home we went on our first date. Our first date turned into many more and eventually I knew I had to tell him. When I did, he was caring, loving, and supportive. He was gentle with me. He let me cry when I needed and held me with warmth and strength. I felt safe with him, and he held my secret as lovingly as he held my heart. We married, had three beautiful children. He was, and always will be, my forever.

When my youngest was in Kindergarten, I decided to fulfill my lifelong dream of becoming a teacher. I entered Millersville University, on Academic probation, at the age of 32. A few years later, after 18 credit semesters, I crossed that stage, diploma in hand, ready to conquer the world. In 2007, I applied to become a Freedom Writer teacher. Erin Gruwell had been a teacher in Long Beach, California, and had been given 150 kids who were labeled as "unteachable", future dropouts, thugs and worse. She did not give up on them and, four years later, all 150 of her students graduated. I wanted to be her. I wanted to help those students that were failing and were hard to reach. On June 16, 2007, I received a phone call from Erin telling me that I had been chosen to train with her in California, along with 20 other teachers from around the United States. I was on cloud nine! I landed in Long Beach, was greeted by Erin with a hug and quickly knew that this experience would change my life. Throughout the next five days, we became Erin's students. We learned how to engage, enlighten and empower our students to become all they could be. But one lesson would change me forever. It is called the Line Game. The twenty teachers, along with a few of the original Freedom Writer students, were taken into a room with a piece of tape dividing the room in half. We each took a side and waited. Erin began asking questions of us, and if it pertained, we would step to the line.

Step to the line if you like pickles.

Step to the line if you like country music.

Step to the line if you are going to a concert this summer. Step to the line if you are going to the beach this summer. Step to the line if you like to dance.

Step to the line if you have ever been to Disney World or Disney Land

Then things got a little different and you could see the mood shift almost immediately.

Step to the line if you were ever made fun of because of who you are. Step to the line if you have been wrongly judged by others.

Step to the line if you know someone who is suffering from an addiction. Step to the line if you know someone who has been homeless.

Step to the line if you know someone who has lost their life to violence.

Step to the line if you know someone who has been abused.

And then it happened. The question I did not want to hear came from Erin's mouth and landed in my throat...

Step to the line if you know someone who has been raped.

I felt like everyone was looking at me, yet no one knew my secret. I waited.

I watched. I was scared. Suddenly, to my right, a beautiful young woman, an original Freedom writer, stood on the line. She was by herself. Tears were streaming down my face. Should I join her on that line? Since the age of 18, only one person had known of my secret. What should I do? Should I own it? Should I continue to run from it? I looked around. The room was quiet. One foot went forward, then another, and before I knew it, I was on the line, crying and shaking. There were two of us. I was not alone. We held each other's hands and cried together, in front of everyone, but we were not alone. We had each other. I was no longer holding a secret. I was almost free, but I was still a prisoner of my past.

In August of 2008, Erin Gruwell invited all the Freedom Writer teachers back to California. At this time, there were 150 of us around the world. We were told during our symposium that we were going to write a book and each of us would have our own entry, mimicking the original *Freedom Writer Diary* that was published in 1999, called *Teaching Hope*. When I submitted my first draft, I received a call from Sue Ellen, an original Freedom Writer student who was now working at the Foundation. This is what happened next:

Hi Anne, It's Sue Ellen!

Hi Sue Ellen! How did you like my piece for the book?

The next words that came from her soft-spoken soul were not what I was expecting!

Anne, anyone could have written that! You know what you need to write! What? That piece was so me! Nobody else could have written that! That was a day in the life of my classroom, nobody else's!

Anne, listen to me. I know it's going to be hard, believe me, I know, but you need to write about your rape.

My heart sank. Sue Ellen was right. What happened to me in college was still haunting me and I needed to write about it.

Okay, I hesitantly said, I will do it, but it won't be easy.

I hung up the phone and my whole body was shaking. How was I going to take so many emotions, thoughts and unimaginable pain and transcribe that one event onto paper? I grabbed my computer and allowed streams of consciousness to overcome my hands as I slowly composed my story. I had sheltered those thoughts for so long that when I saw them in print it made my rape a reality. A heart-breaking, life-changing reality.

I had begun talking about my rape, but writing about it made it more real, more visible. Written words are powerful, spoken words are invisible. I knew that once I wrote my story it could never be taken away. *Teaching Hope* was published in August of 2009, with the story of my rape in black and white. My story was printed but each entry was written anonymously, allowing each of us to take ownership of our own entry, if we chose to do so.

When the book was published, there was one person who was the proudest of me... my father. He picked up the phone and called every relative and friend he could think of to let them know that his "Annie" was an author. How was I going to tell my dad which one was my entry? Almost 30 years had passed and I never told my parents that I was raped as a freshman in college. What would I say and, most importantly, what would he say? My father has always been the one person I could count on to tell me what I needed to hear, not what I wanted to hear. He is the one person I looked to as a role model, an inspiration, a guide that leads with a soft heart and a disciplined soul. I knew this would break his heart.

My dad had been volunteering in my classroom, mentoring a group of my students as they ventured their way through high school. He came alive when he was in my classroom, and my students loved when he would visit. I decided that this was the safest place to let him read my entry. My students met him at the door, and brought him to my classroom. As he entered, my heart was breaking. I knew I was about to tell him something that would tear him apart. Two of my students escorted my dad to his seat, and immediately recited a prayer asking for patience, understanding and healing. My father looked confused and worried. I then began my practiced speech:

Dad, today is going to be a little different. Today is a day that I never wanted to come, but I have no choice anymore. As you know, I have co-authored Teaching Hope and my entry is not signed. We are all anonymous, yet, I want you to know which one is mine. I took my father by his hand and led him to my desk where my story was waiting. Before he started to read, he looked at me with worried eyes and said, "Please tell me you don't have cancer."

"I promise, Dad, I don't have cancer."

With silence, he tilted his head down and began to read. I could see his shoulders tense. I witnessed a transformation of my stoic and strong father into a person who looked lost and heartbroken. He looked up at me and, with sadness and tears in his eyes, he said, "Why didn't you tell me?"

"I couldn't", I struggled to say. "No", he said, "you wouldn't."

Suddenly the class bell rang and the kids, slowly and cautiously, came up to my father and gave him hugs as each of them cried. They then hugged me tightly as they headed out the door. It was now just the two of us.

I didn't know what to do next. But as always, my father knew exactly what to do. He held me. He held me so long I didn't want to let him go. We cried together as we both grieved and accepted what happened to me when I was eighteen years old. I took a deep and cleansing breath, realizing I was finally free.

As I walked my father out of the building, his tears could not be stopped as he said to me, "I have always loved you and I have always been proud of you but I had no idea how strong of a person you really were until today. I admire you for so many reasons, but I admire you mostly for being the person you are today and all that you have gone through. You suffered on your own. You survived on your own. You are stronger than I ever thought. I love you, Dawd."

Rape changes a person. Rape takes away all innocence from a person. Rape owned me for a very long time. But today I am free. I still remember that night like it was yesterday. I still remember the smell of booze, the smell of the vacant room where I became a victim. When Bohemian Rhapsody comes on the radio, it is quickly turned off. I have fears of things that I do not even understand. I have a fear of being alone with strangers and I do not like walking by myself at night whether it be parking lots or the quiet streets of my neighborhood. I find myself looking over my shoulder more often than I care to admit. I am overly cautious and uncertain. I will never drink Jack Daniels again, the memories of those years still fuzzy, yet very clear. I have recurring issues of self-doubt and self-confidence. But, I am becoming stronger every day.

I realized that through writing I was healing myself. Seeing my story on paper allowed me to have control of it. I could choose to rip it to shreds or publish for the world to see. I could keep it my secret forever and hold on to the past, or write it with my heart and allow myself to slowly regain who I am. I chose to write. I chose to take control of my life and own my past. I chose to heal myself through writing. It was not easy. It did not happen quickly and it did not end with my first writing. Each day I continue to heal. Each day I choose to live in the present and let go of the past. However, it is still a part of me. But, I can now say that I am stronger because I have claimed it as MY story.

Ten years ago, I was asked a question: "Who are you? You seem to be so put together, yet there is something hidden behind your smile." Today I would respond a bit differently. I would stand strong and proud and say:

I am what I am. I am Virginia Ann Marie Penny Schober. I am a different name to different people but I am the same person. I am a daughter, a wife, a mother, a sister, a friend. I was a rape victim, but I am now a survivor.

I am what I am but I am not what happened to me. I am a fighter who fights invisible fears and harsh realities. I am a survivor who has overcome and yet lived to tell my story. I am a victim that was in a fight and lost, and that is okay. I am a person that can look back on what happened to me with sadness rather than hate. I am a person that can look forward with hope rather than despair. I am a person that may never forget, but does not need to constantly remember. I am not what happened to me, but I am what I choose to become. I am a voice that needs to be heard and will not allow the silence that once engulfed me to return. I am a person who stands for victims in hopes that they will see themselves as survivors. I am a person of scars, and each scar tells a story. I am the owner of my story and that is the bravest thing I will ever do. I am what I am. I am Virginia Anne Marie Penny Schober. I am strong. I am hopeful. I am determined. I am free.

A special young man, Zach W., recently wrote: "Writing helps me calm myself. It helps me discover who I am and where I belong. Sometimes I feel angry and lost and writing helps me to put my feelings into words. It helps to tell my story."

Who are you? What story do you need to tell? What parts of your life do you need to explore? What is holding you back?

Let's begin this writing journey knowing that you have much to tell!

Anne

Lisa

While growing up, I remember processing my life through writing. Paper and pen beckoned to me, perhaps the way a cell phone calls out to today's teens. Journal entry, simple poem, note to a friend - somehow written words proved I existed, that my experience was real. As an adult, I continue to find that the physical and mental act of putting words to the page helps to untangle my web of thoughts and emotions. **Yet still I hesitate to call** myself a "writer." (Oh, the lengths we go to as women to keep ourselves in a humble place, to hold ourselves "back.")

One truth I have learned in writing is that poems unlock power. They reach into our unconscious and tug at the strands of our lives that beg for words. While working with sixth graders, I have noticed that providing a running start for their poetry writing provides a springboard for what is inside of them. Giving a lifted line from another poem can send their writing in a direction that leaves our classroom community speechless with awe, or sharing in the writer's raw tears.

Here is one running start we have used – it has borrowed lines from another student's poem (which comes from the book _100 Quickwrites by Linda Rief_).

What is it about my grandpa? That makes me break down sobbing.

For one of my students, these lines became...

> _What is it about my sister?_
> _I used to break down and cry._
> _Is it because I see pictures of her,_
> _and we look exactly alike?_
> _I heard she and I have the same birthday_
> _But I was born a minute before._
> _She may not know about me_
> _But I know about her._
> _All I want to do is meet her._
> _I miss you sis._

Dymir B

The poem becomes the journal entry — and in that vulnerable moment, a sacred space is created.

A single story becomes universal.

It is within these honest stories where healing can begin.

The desire to use writing as a healing endeavor and share strategies with other teachers led me to create a graduate course. After spending time with Anne Schober, I knew from an instinctual space that she was the instructor I wanted by my side to co-teach. And thus, the class, *Writing to Heal, Empower, and Build Community* was born. Later, Anne and I began to offer retreats and workshops outside of the world of education. It was no surprise to find that teachers and other adults, as well as children, can lift lines from poems, and in the process, lift their subconscious minds to a place where healing and empowerment may begin.

The piece I am going to share with you was inspired by a line in another student's poem. While writing about her parents' divorce, she declared…

> *Not my fault*
> *Not my fault*
> *Not my fault.*

For me this became…

> *Not mine,*
> *Not mine,*
> *Not mine.*

I remember for the student, it was a healing poem, for she was able to voice through her writing that she was angry and tired of being caught in the middle of two people she loved.

Like my students who wrote to work through their feelings, the piece I am sharing with you on the next page helped me name a loss and express the emotions that came with it. A time of joy quickly faded into a time of life questioning and depression. Rather than go into detail about my struggles at the time, I will let you read the piece and experience it as it is.

You may want to think about whether journaling in the form of poetry is something that fits with you. Putting words to the page in this way is the format that my friend Donna prefers. You will meet her writing later in this book!

By sharing some of our own pieces here, Anne and I hope you will see writing as something that ordinary people do. We hope you will see where vulnerability, writing, and healing meet.

Life is messy. So is writing. It is only fitting then, that these two should walk hand in hand.

-Lisa

Intricate spiraled beauty
miraculous new life
inside.
Announcing
your presence to others,
my heart
leaps,
Surrounds you with
love.
I gaze upon
the picture
of you
in my womb.
Already
so connected
as I wait,
Already mine.

You are
Too still.
Blood pressure
dropping
Nurse lingering
Too quiet!
Doctor
talking
hospital
What is he saying?
Why
are they taking
You
Away
From me?

Gone.
Alone.
Missing you.
I am empty.

Not mine.
Not mine.
not,
Mine.

Unexpected teen
Movie star model
Sister - younger than me
Everywhere
I look
Women
glowing,
Expectant
with new life.

I wait.
Again disappointed.
Jealous dragon
Don't eat me
As I
watch
And wait.

Not time
Not time
Not time.
Waving my fist
At the
Baby-giving
gods.

And where is
That God of
Mine?
What makes
Mary and Elizabeth
More special than me?

I wait.
I have no choice.

HOW TO USE THIS BOOK
Write what needs to be written.
Erin Gruwell

riting Through the Mess: Seeking Healing Through Writing is divided into three sections: Exploring, Enlightening and Embracing. Each section will feature stories of individuals who have used writing as a cathartic tool in their own lives, as well as writing prompts and exercises, quotes, poems and songs for reflection and listening. There will be some exercises that grab your attention at one moment, and perhaps a story that causes you to ponder your own life in a different section. If you read a line or a phrase that grabs you by the heart, Lift it! Write it in your journal and see where it takes you! This is your book and your own writing experience. Do what is best for you. Find your own meaning in all the mess!

Feel free to read through the book first, if you wish. This way you can get the feel for the book and some ideas might jump out from your first read through. Or, simply trust the process and follow us page by page to begin the journey of healing your heart by exploring, enlightening and embracing yourself. We promise that no matter how you use this book, by allowing yourself to be open to the writing process and listening to what needs to be written, you will begin to discover the power of using writing to heal.

"Let the wild rumpus start."
Maurice Sendak

13

Using a Writer's Notebook/Journal
as a Vehicle to Heal

As Shelley Harwayne so eloquently wrote, "A notebook is a container where we can save and savor observations and ideas." As a person who is about to embark on a very personal writing journey, having your own notebook or journal may be one of the most important tools you will use. It will be a place where you will store your ideas and all your writings throughout this process. What is a writer's notebook or journal?

It is...

- A net to catch ideas.

- A map that leads you back to people and events from your life.

- A scrapbook and a garbage bag where you gather goodies, but also junk that won't be used.

- A surfboard where you try different moves, and ride around in ideas.

- A mind reader that helps figure out what is on your mind.

- A way of breathing in and breathing out.

- A vessel that will hold your most precious gift – your words.

- A truth-seeker, daring you to speak the truth, letting you know if you are telling yourself a lie or if you are holding back.

- A mentor that pulls you toward the words you need to write.

- A listening ear, that lets you speak without interruption or outside judgement.

You can choose to use the pages within this book as your journal or purchase a notebook or journal of your pleasing. What is most important is that whatever you choose to hold your words will be a book you feel honored to have and hold dearly in your heart.

Before You Begin

Believe in yourself and the process. As you explore your past and present, you may find that you have more questions and less answers and vice versa. Be open to this concept and accept where you are in the moment. **Trust yourself as you write.** Do not worry about spelling, grammar and word choice. Just write. This is an important part of the writing journey. And, lastly, give yourself permission to **write what needs to be written**. Write from your voice within. Write with your soul and heart.

Barry Lane, a talented writer and educator, begins his workshops by having participants recite an oath. We believe in this so much that we would like you to take an oath, as well.

Raise your right hand and say the following - loudly, boldly, and proudly:

*I swear from this time forward to **explore** the truth, the whole truth and nothing but the truth. As I find **enlightenment**, I will forgive myself for actions in the past and for where I fall short of my expectations. As I write, I will **embrace** my words and where they may lead me. I will **embrace** myself.*

Let's get started!

"Every secret of a writer's soul, every experience of his life, every quality of his mind, is written large in his works."
Virginia Woolf

EXPLORING

"The scariest moment is always just before you start. After that, things can only get better."

Stephen King

Exercise #1 - Creating your Life Graph

"We can chart our future clearly and wisely only when we know the path which has led to the present."
Adlai E. Stevenson

Life Graphs are used to represent the highs and lows of your life. The higher the point, the better the experience; the lower the point, the worse the experience. What better way to start our journey together than by creating your own life graph?

There is no right or wrong way when creating your life graph. You can choose 15 moments or events in your lifetime that are important enough to include in your life graph, or 100! The key is to include both positives and negatives. The highs and the lows are what make us the people we are. On Facebook, you will see mostly positives about people: new dog, new baby, new job, vacation, won a million dollars, etc. Rarely will you see the trials that occur daily (however, we all know that **one** person who posts EVERYTHING!). The key to keep in mind is whether the events you are graphing are important to you in some way.

For example, some key points on my life graph would include: the births of my three children, my mother's death, my father's cancer, the marriage of my daughter, the birth of my grandson, etc. Highs and lows – all very important to who I am.

Directions: Draw a line across the middle of the page (horizontally is best). Begin graphing by placing your high points ABOVE the line and the low points BELOW the line. It is best to do this in chronological order. Remember… the higher the point on the graph, the better the experience!

Each individual day that we are given is filled with high moments and low moments. Even in one day, we have experienced a multitude of both. You may also want to try to zoom in on "a day in the life" to do a separate graph. What are the highs and lows you experience in a day? This exercise can lead you to those issues that have been simmering, but also to small moments of gratitude.

Use a variety of colors if you want. This is your experience, your journey, your story!

"Feelings are like a color chart that God has given us."
Keith Miller

Graph It!

who are you really?

you are not a name
or a height, or a weight
or a gender
you are not an age
and you are not where you are
from

you are your favorite books
and the songs stuck in your
head
you are your thoughts
and what you eat for breakfast
on Saturday mornings

you are a thousand things
but everyone chooses
to see the million things
you are not

you are not
where you are from
you are
where you are going
and i'd like
to go there
too

M.K.

Exercise #2 - I Am What I Am

*"I took a deep breath and listened to the brag of my
heart; I am, I am, I am."*
Sylvia Plath

Who are you? Sounds simple enough, but it can be the most daunting question you are asked. We are so many things to so many people, yet we are the same person inside. We are complex, yet simple. We are splendid, yet ordinary. We are what we are!

Step One: Draw a head on your page. It can be as detailed or as simple as you wish.

Step Two: In the white space OUTSIDE the head, write words that describe who you are on the outside. Words that people would use to describe you from physically seeing you. For example: tall, short, female, male, athletic, curvy, thin, blonde, brunette, etc. Fill the white space with as many words as possible. Spend as much time as possible discovering words that describe you. If possible, write for at least 3-5 minutes.

Step Three: On the INSIDE of the head, write words that describe who you are on the inside. These are the qualities and characteristics that are **not** visible to others. These traits are the core of YOU. Example words: strong, empathetic, depressed, moral, complex, weak, uncertain, valued - anything goes. Write as many words as possible... Fill the Head! Spend five or more minutes discovering the words that really define you as a person.

Step Four: Once you have a "full head," highlight or circle the words that stand out to you. The strong words – the ones that speak to you! If you have a yellow highlighter, use it! The words you highlight will be called your GOLDEN WORDS.

Step Five: Write the words "I Am What I Am." Begin writing using the words "I am what I am" and go where the muse leads. Use your "golden words" to guide you through this writing piece. If you need some ideas, go back to the beginning of the book and read over Anne's piece. Lift words, lines, phrases – whatever you need to get started. There is no right or wrong way to write this piece. Repeat the phrase "I am what I am" as much as you feel necessary. Who are you?

*"You'll never know who you are unless you shed
who you pretend to be."*
Vironika Tugaleva

Who Are You?

I Am What I Am

Exercise #3 - When I Was Young at the Ocean
"For the writer, there is no oblivion. Only endless memory."
Anita Brookner

This writing prompt is going to take you back to a special time in your childhood. Time spent at the mountains, the beach, the lake, or your grandparents' home can conjure memories that will be forever etched in your mind, memories from your childhood that make you smile and your heart dance. Maybe your memories are from a vacation with your entire family at the beach, hiking the mountains, growing up in the Bronx, or being raised on the farm. Whatever those memories are for you, they are special. Getting in touch with those grounding places and moments from your past help you heal because you can be in touch with those forces that help you feel anchored and in harmony.

Step One: Take a few minutes and jot down special memories of when you were young. Make a list and try to include as many memories as possible, including as much detail as you can remember. If this is too broad for you, try narrowing it down to a specific age range (for example, ages 6-8).

Step Two: Read the following imagery piece by Linda Rief. While reading, concentrate on the language she uses and the images she is portraying while capturing this childhood memory.

When I Was Young at the Ocean by Linda Rief

When I was young at the ocean, I sat at the edge of the wooden pier and dangled my toes in the water. Like tiny rowboats my toes skimmed the rolling waves, ever alert for sharks. Sometimes I sat cross-legged in shorts and tee-shirt, a bamboo fishing pole stretched to catch mackerel. No one ever told me to bait the hook.

When I was young at the ocean, I cracked open mussels and periwinkles and clams, and ran my fingers across their gushy insides. I squished seaweed nodules between my forefinger and thumb, anxious for the pop and spray from the moist insides.

When I was young at the ocean, I burned my shoulders and smelled like Noxzema through the entire month of July. I drank in the aroma of hip roses, salt water, and seaweed. At low tide I played croquet with the Queen of Hearts, flew to the moon in a hammock, and fed my dolls deviled ham sandwiches in the shade of the screened house.

As the tide came in, water lapped at the rocky shore. The skin of my feet toughened as I paced those rounded stones, my eyes searching for skippers. *When I was young, I never wished to climb the mountains, or live in the city, or camp in the forest. The ocean was enough. It still is.*

Step Three: Pick one of your favorite memories you listed earlier and, using the style of Linda Reif, write about that special time in your life. Begin each new paragraph with the words, "When I was young at the ....". Use as much description as you can, remembering details, smells, sounds, and sights that draw you back to that particular memory. Focus on specific nouns and verbs rather than strings of adjectives. Remember, "Lift a line" if you need to jumpstart your writing!

"To live is the rarest thing in the world. Most people exist, that is all."
Oscar Wilde

When I Was Young

Exercise #4 - Heart Maps

"Fill your paper with breathings from the heart."
William Wordsworth

Have you ever heard of heart maps? A heart map is a visual representation of what a person loves or cares about. This heart-shaped picture uses drawings and words to show the things that "live" in a person's heart, waiting for the chance to be revealed by a writing activity. The most important ideas go in the middle and the less important things go in the surrounding spaces.

First mentioned by Georgia Heard in her book *Awakening the Heart,* heart maps can help writers attend to writing from a much deeper level than most prompts. Sometimes, it is easier to express yourself more accurately and completely when you use this visual display.

Step One: Gather some colored pencils, markers or crayons.

Step Two: Draw a large heart in the center of the page. The bigger the better!

Step Three: Think of the following questions:

- What has stayed in your heart?
- What memories, moments, people, animals, objects, places, books, fears, scars, friends, siblings, parents, grandparents, teachers, other people, journeys, secrets, dreams, crushes, relationships, comforts, and learning experiences live in your heart?
- What small things/moments are important to you?
- What dreams do you hold dear to your heart?
- What or who should be at the center of your heart? The edges?
- *What is in your heart?*

Step Four: Begin filling in your heart. You can do this any way you choose, it is your heart. You can use colors to categorize your items. For example: red for people, purple for activities, green for places, yellow for emotions, etc. Be creative and have fun exploring your heart!"

The idea is to write it so that people hear it and it slides through the brainand goes straight to the heart."
Maya Angelou

In My Heart

Exercise #5 - Silent Reflection

"An awake heart is like a sky that pours light."
Hafel

Step One: Sit silently for twenty minutes; no music, conversation, reading or writing. Take inventory of the feelings in your heart. Consider why these feelings are coming up.

Step Two: After twenty minutes, write what needs to be written.

"The writer presents himself to the blank page not with an open passport but an open heart."
Taiye Selasi

My Silent Inventory

FORKED BRANCHES
Suzy Kassem

We grew up on the same street,
You and me.
We went to the same schools,
Rode the same bus,
Had the same friends,
And even shared spaghetti
With each other's families.

And though our roots belong to
The same tree,
Our branches have grown
In different directions.
Our tree,
Now resembles a thousand
Other trees
In a sea of a trillion
Other trees
With parallel destinies
And similar dreams.
You cannot envy the branch
That grows bigger
From the same seed,
And you cannot
Blame it on the sun's direction.
But you still compare us,
As if we're still those two
Kids at the park
Slurping down slushies and
Eating ice cream.

Minor Snobs
Daniel Amory

Shortly before school started, I moved into a studio apartment on a quiet street near the bustle of the downtown in one of the most self-conscious bends of the world. The "Gold Coast" was a neighborhood that stretched five blocks along the lake in a sliver of land just south of Lincoln Park and north of River North. The streets were like fine necklaces and strung together were the brownstone houses and tall condominiums and tiny mansions like pearls, and when the day broke and the sun faded away, their lights burned like jewels shining gaudily in the night. The world's most elegant bazaar, Michigan Avenue, jutted out from its eastern tip near The Drake Hotel and the timeless blue-green waters of Lake Michigan pressed its shores. The fractious make-up of the people that inhabited it, the flat squareness of its parks and the hint of the lake at the ends of its tree-lined streets squeezed together a domesticated cesspool of age and wealth and standing. It was a place one could readily dress up for an expensive dinner at one of the fashionable restaurants or have a drink miles high in the lounge of the looming John Hancock Building and five minutes later be out walking on the beach with pants cuffed and feet in the cool water at the lake's edge.

Exercise #6 - Neighborhood Maps

"Don't forget to leave your handprints on the ones you love and your footprints around the neighborhood."
Lisa Miller

Sometimes jumping in with both feet is the best way to write! And, sometimes we need a little help by using art to capture memories. For this activity, you will be doing a little bit of both! This exercise is simple and yet can generate more stories, memories, laughter and tears than imagined. Sometimes, our childhood is filled with emotions and events that we have locked away in our memory for a long time. Allowing yourself to delve into your past can be the first step to exploring who you are. Be open to where this activity leads you.

Step One: Gather colored pencils, markers, or crayons, if you wish.

Step Two: What is your answer when you are asked the question, "Where did you grow up?" Is it the family home you were born in? Is it the place you lived for only a few years? Is it an apartment? A row home? A farm? A house in a suburban neighborhood? Wherever that place is to you, close your eyes and think of as many details as you can.

Step Three: Draw a map of your neighborhood. Include street names, landmarks, parks, secret hiding spots, places you use to "hang out", stores, etc. Think of the people you were with, where they lived, neighbors, even the neighbor that everyone feared! Think of as many details as you can and draw them in your map. No detail is too small and no memory too insignificant.

Step Four: By looking at your map, what stories have you discovered? What memories make you smile? Cry? Laugh? Which memory/memories call you to explore it/them on a different level? If needed, share your map with someone and have them tell you which story or stories they want to know more about.

Step Five: Then, begin writing! Include details, emotions, scents, feelings and whatever you need to capture your story. Go back to your map, as needed, to rediscover your story.

"True navigation begins in the human heart. It is the most important map of all."
Elizabeth Lindsey

My Neighborhood Map

My Memories

Exercise #7 - I Come From

A poem by George Ella Lyon called "Where I'm From" has been used many times over for creating a beautiful piece of exploration and belonging. And we hope that you will give it a try. Where we come from is the core of who we are and exploring this idea can lead us to questions and answers we never expected.

Step One: Read the original poem by George Lyon below. Examine his use of words, details, and sounds.

Step Two: Following the poem, you will see a template that you can use to write your own "I Come From" poem in the same format as Mr. Lyon. The prompts have a way of drawing out memories of the smells of attics and bottom-drawer keepsakes; the faces of long-departed kin, the sound of their voices you still hold some deep place in memory. You'll be surprised that, when you are done, you will have said things about the sources of your uniqueness that you might not have considered before.

Step Three: If you choose, you can take your writing further. Following the template, you will see "I Come From" written by Lisa. She has used the idea of the "I Am From" poem and adapted it to write a piece more elaborate and personal. By repeating the words, "I Come From," you can write your own piece imitating Lisa's style. Remember that you can "lift a line," a word or an idea.

Who are you and where are you from?

Where I'm From By George Ella Lyon

I am from clothespins,
from Clorox and carbon-tetrachloride.
I am from the dirt under the back porch. (Black,
glistening
it tasted like beets.)
I am from the forsythia bush,
the Dutch elm
whose long gone limbs I remember
as if they were my own.
I am from fudge and eyeglasses,
from Imogene and Alafair.
I'm from the know-it-alls
and the pass-it-ons,
from perk up and pipe down. I'm
from He restoreth my soul with
cottonball lamb
and ten verses I can say myself.
I'm from Artemus and Billie's Branch,
fried corn and strong coffee. From the
finger my grandfather lost to the auger,
the eye my father shut to keep his sight.
Under my bed was a dress box
spilling old pictures.
a sift of lost faces
to drift beneath my dreams. I am
from those moments – snapped
before I budded – leaf-fall from the
family tree.

I Am From Template

I am from _____ (specific
ordinary item), from _____
__ (product name) and _____.

I am from the _____
_____ (home description) (adjective, adjective, sensory detail).

I am from the _____
_____ (plant, flower, natural item), the _____
_____ (plant, flower, natural detail).

I am from _____ (family tradition)
and _____ (family trait), from
_____ _ (name of family member)
and _____ (another family name)
and _____ (family name).

I am from the _____
_____ (description of family tendency)
and _____ (another one).

From _____ (something you were told as
a child) and_____ (another).

I am from (representation of religion, or lack of it).
Further description.

I'm from _____ (place of birth
and family ancestry), and _____
(two food items representing your family).

From the _____ (specific family
story about a specific person and detail), the_____
_____ (another detail), and the_____
_____ (another detail about another family member).

I am from_____ (location
of family pictures, mementos, archives and several more lines
indicating their worth).

I Come From – Lisa Roth Walter

I come from the rugged rocks of the West Coast, the rainbow umbrellas of the soft Eastern shore, and a mother who connected the two worlds by reading Laura Ingalls Wilder as we drove our station wagon along the shimmering paved roads that replaced the wagon ruts of the past, crossing the country on the Oregon Trail.

I come from Mennonite hymns, banana bread, wet Grandma Shirk kisses, and tearful laughter – as we surrounded the death-bed of our family's beloved matriarch.

I come from many greens: The deep mossy green of Oregon, the waxy dark green of Kenya's coffee trees, the blackened green sky of Indiana's tornado alley, and the bright lime green of Mexican margaritas when the college gals turned 40. Tequila!

I come from the humanitarian acts of Mother Teresa, Princess Diana, Martin Luther King, Jr., and Gandhi. I come from their peaceful searches for justice, and their touches of the needy. I come from the belief that love and nonviolence can be the most powerful forces on this Earth. I come from the desire to share these truths of life with my sixth grade students.

I come from the frenzied balancing act of motherhood and career pursuits. I come from course proposals, graduate credits, daily discipline, and curricular creations. I also come from peanut butter and jelly, homework helping, watching soccer, and staring at the messy kitchen – again. Through conversations on the run with my husband, I maneuver this mid-life ride.

I come from quiet found in good-night chats with my children, the gentle listening ears of my parents, shared beach confidences with friends and late night solitude.

I come from centered calm and complete chaos.

I come from the created collage of life in and around me.

I Come From

Exercise #8 - Promise

"There is promise in every new dawn. Promise of a new start, new chances, new opportunities and new hope. Always remember the promise."
Doe Zantamata

As children, many times we made "pinky promises" with our best friends, a sign of secrets and trust. Having a "pinky promise" is a special bond which brings with it a strong sense of faith between friends. Did you ever make a "pinky promise" when you were little? Did you ever "cross my heart and hope to die, put a needle in my eye?" Did you ever make a promise with someone and then discover they have broken your trust?

As an adult, I still find myself making "pinky promises" with friends, both old and young. It is a promise to see each other soon, a promise to never forget how much fun we had, or a promise to always be there for each other. The significance of a "pinky promise" still holds strong today as it did so many years ago.

Step One: Read the following poem and reflection by Danielle.

Step Two: What memories immediately come into picture from your own childhood? What images are drifting through your heart and mind? Maybe you made a promise with someone and you broke the promise? Maybe someone you trusted broke a promise you shared with them? Write down all that you are thinking, remembering and feeling using your stream of consciousness to take you away....

"Sometimes people don't understand the promises they are making when they make them, I said. Isaac shot me a look. Right, of course. But you keep the promise anyway. That is what love is. Love is keeping the promise anyway. Don't you believe in true love?"
John Green, The Fault in Our Stars

Pinky Promise
Danielle N.

"Let's promise to never be like them."
My 12 year-old self said,
"Pinky Promise, everyone,
Let's promise...
We'll never turn out that way. We'll
never make our kids scared We'll
never put them in danger. Our kids
will never see us being hit.
Our kids will never wonder where their next
meal will come from.
We will be different.
We will do different.
Please before we are separated, let's promise
Right here, right now."

We peered through
The window and watched
The happy laughter That could turn…
…We had seen it turn. We had felt that wrath.
We had been caught in the illusion
That everything was well.
And then snap…

The wrong thing was said
And the tensions mounted…

Kids don't understand The history of adults
They don't understand
The weight attached to words.
And history goes back a long way. Further than we could
understand.

That's why we must promise to not
Turn out like them…

All of our pinkies hooked,
We looked solemnly in each other's eyes
Vowing with our hearts, Believing that words and pinkies would
Make the promise come true.

We didn't yet understand how history can repeat itself, How you
can mean something with all your heart And still not keep your
promise.

This is the pinky promise of addiction.

Writing has helped me get clarity about different aspects of my life and understand it more deeply. It has allowed me to move from blame to compassion for both myself and for those most dear to me. Before exploring my youth through writing, I often vacillated between anger and victimization. When revisiting my childhood through writing, I have been able to dig deeper into my real feelings and emotions. I have also been given the gift of time healing old wounds. Now that I have acknowledged these difficult times, I have been able to heal and move forward. Uncensored free writing prompts where I am just given permission and encouraged to just write has allowed me to write now and ask questions later.

When writing "Pinky Promises" I started with a distinct memory of the day I moved from my childhood home. Before leaving, we made a promise to one another that we would not go down the same paths our loved ones had gone down. As children, we felt like we stuck together and helped each other through those times. We made this pact because that's the only thing we could do to try to keep each other safe now that we wouldn't be together anymore. Pinky promises were such binding contracts in my childhood and I meant my promise with all my heart that day, but it was not too many years later that I struggled down a troubled road. Even something as serious as a pinky promise couldn't overcome the power of addiction.

Danielle N.

Promises

Exercise #9 - Scavenger Hunt

"Your heart is where your treasure is, and you must find your treasure in order to make sense of everything."
Paulo Coehlo

One of my favorite birthday parties when I was a little girl was a Scavenger Hunt that my parents designed for me. They sent me and my best friends on a search around the neighborhood looking for treasures on our sacred lists. Looking for items while laughing through our search is a memory I will forever cherish. That is the idea behind this fun and whimsical activity.

The goal of this particular scavenger hunt is to hunt for images — or things that appeal to your senses. Images that strike you. That surprise you. That please you. Images you want to remember. Or, simply, images you like.

Step One: Gather scissors, glue, tape, markers, and coloring pencils.

Step Two: Forage your house, office place, doctor's office, bookshelves and trash cans for magazines, newspapers, catalogs, inserts, books of poetry or children's books, old photographs, and any printed material including your own written material from journals.

Step Three: Go on a hunt for images, words and phrases that strike you. Images that make you smile. Words that you want to use in your own writing. Images that remind you of a special time or place. Words that tug at your heart. If you have ever written down any of your dreams, these can be an excellent source of images. Your memory can also be a source of images. Songs. Movies. Overheard conversation. The possibilities are endless.

Step Four: Fill a page or two or three with the images and words you found. Try to leave as little white space as possible, creating a collage of thoughts, ideas and images.

Step Five: After your page(s) are complete, reflect on your final product. Maybe you will make a list of images and words. Perhaps you will write about a particular image. The choice is up to you. What did you discover about yourself as you were going on your scavenger hunt? Try giving your collection of images a name. You may want to try having a conversation with your collage. This is a technique used by people who make SoulCollages. It can help you think deeply about the images you have collected and the connections they may have with each other.

Ask the collage, "Who are you?"

Write the answer from the collage's viewpoint. "I am one who..."
Ask the collage, "What do you have to give me?"

Write the answer from the collage's viewpoint. "I give you..." Ask the collage, "What do you want from me?"

Write the answer from the collage's viewpoint. "I want you to...

Here is a SoulCollage made by Lisa, and her answers to the questions.

Title: African Childhood

Who are you?

I am one who is your African childhood. I am one who plays a regular childhood in an irregular place. I am one who carries the beat of a village drum. I am one who integrates past with present.

What do you have to give me?

Like the drum, I give you life's rhythms. I give you freedom for free play like your African childhood.

What do you want from me?

I want you to integrate the past for present compassion. I want you to hold memories and wisdom from the past, and yet let go to step into the present and future. I want you to feel the beauty in the rhythm of life's cycles.

Images

SoulCollage

Exercise #10 - Musical Interlude

"Where words fail, music speaks."
Hans Christian Anderson

It's been said that music is the universal language. Whether you enjoy classical, country, blues, jazz, pop, hip hop or classic rock, music is magical. Music is healing. Music can take a rainy day and turn it into sunshine and rainbows. Music can soothe your soul when nothing else can.

At this point in your writing, it is time to take a step back, relax and listen. Listen to your heart. Listen to what your inner muse is trying to say. Listen to the quiet that is trying to escape. Take this time to simply listen. Find your favorite musical piece, play it softly in the background, or sit in complete silence. What is important is to breathe, relax and listen with no interruptions.

Step One: Find a quiet place and take your journal/book with you.

Step Two: Sit quietly and, if you choose, play your favorite music.

Step Three: Listen.

Step Four: Write as much or as little as you need to at this particular moment.

"Silence is the most powerful scream."
Unknown

Exercise #11 - Questioning

*"Courage doesn't happen when you have all the answers.
It happens when you are ready to face the questions
you have been avoiding your whole life."*
Shannon L. Alder

Sometimes all it takes to recall a memory, to explore who we are, is a question. The question can be simple, complex, intriguing, or compelling. Sometimes the right question can help discover an answer that has been eluding our minds and soul.

Directions: Read the list of questions that follow and answer the ones that speak to you. Maybe you will feel ready to jump into one question right away or sit and ponder another question for a few minutes, hours or days. This is your journey. Explore your answers. At your own pace.

Questions:

When did you become an adult? How do people change?

Who were you?

Is the night sky the same as when you were a child?

What is a dream you have?

Are you holding on to something you need to let go?

When was the last time you noticed the sound of your own breathing?

How old would you be if you didn't know how old you are?

What is the last thing you have done that is really worth remembering?

What are your pretending not to know?

What else?

Exploring Questions

Exercise #12 - Revisit

"An unresolved past never really goes away until you find the courage to revisit all the pain and accept that there is nothing you can do to change the past. What's happened has happened, and what is done is done."
Unknown

Before moving on to the next section, take the time and revisit what you have written. Maybe there is a question you need to explore further. Maybe you left a writing piece half-written and you want to finish. Maybe you wrote something so powerful that you need to go back and re-read your entry. Maybe you just need to reflect on what you have written, where you have been and where you are going.

It is important to revisit. It is important to pause. It is important to reflect.

Step One: Revisit your pages of writing, reading and reflecting as you go.

Step Two: Add to your writing, if necessary. Take a "golden line" from one of your writing pieces, lift it, and begin a new piece. Write questions that you may want to explore more deeply. Whatever you need to do, do it. Be sure to revisit each of your pieces and look deeply into your words by exploring who you are.

"I'm afraid that the gift of visiting the past is all that we have. We can revisit it, but only as it happened."
Karen Essex

Golden Line Revisited

ENLIGHTENING

"To enjoy good health, to bring true happiness to one's family, to bring peace to all, one must first discipline and control one's own mind. If a man can control his mind he can find the way to Enlightenment, and all wisdom and virtue will naturally come to him."
Buddha

Exercise #13- Through the Looking Glass (Part One)

*"Dear you, make peace with the mirror
and watch your reflection change."*
Unknown

"Can you look at this from my point of view?" Maybe this question has been asked of you. If so, what was your reaction? What made it hard or easy to respond? Either way, looking at ourselves as others see us is important to fully understand who we are. By doing so, we are enlightening ourselves.

Step One: List ten people that you have "disliked" at one point in your life. No one is off limits.

Step Two: Pick ONE of the people you have listed and write ten things you dislike about that person. Try to pick a person that causes you to emit a lot of different emotions, if possible.

Step Three: Pretend you are the person you just wrote about. Now, list ten things that person does not like about you.

Step Four: Go over both lists and look for similarities. Highlight the traits you have in common or create a new list. Pretend you are the other person. Start with this line: "Can you look at this from my point of view?"

Step Five: Did you realize the similarities before you began this exercise? What did you learn about yourself from the other person's point of view? What did you learn about the other person?

*"In a mirror we find a reflection of our appearances,
but in heart we find a reflection of our soul."*
Unknown

A Different Point of View

Exercise #14- Through the Looking Glass (Part Two)

"You are so much more than what you see in the mirror,"
Unknown

"You walk like a duck." "You look like a toothpick."

"You don't have any friends because you stink." "You are so stupid."

"You look like a beached whale." "You have a big butt."

Words hurt. And sometimes we take these negative words we hear and turn them into truths, believing everything we hear. It has been said that you can give a person many, many compliments, but give them one negative comment and that is what they remember. What names have you been called? What words have you heard that still pierce your heart? Who made fun of you? Were you ever bullied? What false rumors were spread about you?

Thinking back on the rough times in your life is difficult, but it is vital in moving forward. Discovering your own weaknesses can help you to become strong.

Step One: Write down the names of people who have made fun of you, said mean things about you, started rumors about you and have hurt your feelings. These people can be family, friends, co-workers, etc. As you are writing, try to remember what words were spoken by each person. Take the time to write the backstory.

Step Two: Reflect on the words that were once said of you. If you can, find a secluded area and scream (or say loudly) the words that hurt your feelings. In doing so, try to release those words from your heart once and for all. As you say (or scream) the words out loud, what are you feeling? What memories does this activity evoke?

Step Three: Let's take this activity one step further. Write down a few of your personal weaknesses. For example: low self-esteem, close-minded, lazy, impatient, self-critical.

Step Four: Reflect on your list. What can you do to turn these weaknesses into positives? How have the negative words others have said influenced how you feel about yourself? If possible, once again find a secluded area and scream out your weaknesses into the universe. Free yourself from the negatives that have clouded your thinking. Write about what you have learned about yourself through this exercise.

"You cannot change how people treat you or what they say about you.
All you can do is change how you react to it."
Unknown

Letting Go

Exercise #15- Two Voices Poem

In the first two activities of this section, you were asked to look "Through the Looking Glass" at yourself through the eyes of others, and through your own. Examining who you are is a difficult road and conjures up memories which can create a variety of emotions. The Two Voices Poem will be the next step in letting go.

A poem in two voices offers a unique way to showcase two distinct perspectives or to compare and contrast two items or people. The two voices go back and forth so that it becomes a dialogue or conversation. If the poet wants the voices to come together as one, the words are either written in the center of the page or on the same line in each of the two columns.

Step One: Read over the first two activities and your journal entries in the *Enlightening* section.

Step Two: Read the example which follows and create your own Two Voices Poem by penning two columns of dialogue between yourself and someone else. The very simple poem below is about a thirty-year friendship which ended.

Other Ideas: One column can be the negatives people have said about you, with the second column being the positives or the affirmations you are telling yourself. Or, one column can be the person you wrote about who you dislike, the second column can be your perspective, and the things you have in common can be in the middle. Another option is to have both voices be your own the ones suggested in the quote by Charles Newcomb. Try having one voice be the voice of fear, and the other voice be the whisper of your higher self.

Two Voices Poem
Anne Schober

You never listen to me.   You were not there for me when
                                                 I needed you most.

We have been friends for over 30 years.

We once shared secrets that were only ours.   You became someone
                                                 I no longer knew.

Our friendship began to crumble.

When I met someone new,   You neglected our friendship
you abandoned me.   while forging a new relationship.

Nothing lasts forever.

I miss you. I miss your laugh. I miss your smile.   I miss the person
                                                         you were.

I don't know what else to say.
I am sorry.

Two Voices

Exercise #16- Digging Deeper

"It would be easy to become a victim of our circumstances and continue feeling sad, scared or angry; or instead, we could choose to deal with injustice humanely and break the chains of negative thoughts and energies, and not let ourselves sink into it."
Erin Gruwell, The Freedom Writers Diary

When Anne went through the process of becoming a Freedom Writer Teacher, she never knew how impactful a question could be. When she was asked, "Do you know someone who has been raped?" her world changed forever. No one had ever asked her that question and, if they had, she would never have felt comfortable answering. Anne was raped, but she never chose to accept that reality until she could answer honestly. Once she did, her heart began to heal.

Instructions:

Step One: Read over each question thoughtfully. If the answer to the question is yes, write the question in your notebook with a response following. For example: I do know someone who was raped and that person is me. While it has been over 30 years since it happened, it still feels like yesterday.

Step Two: Write as much or as little as you wish. If you desire, save space between your responses to return at a later date.

Step Three: If you find a question that is too hard to answer thoughtfully and honestly, simply circle it in your workbook and visit it later. Just be sure to return to it.

Step Four: After you make your way through the questions, write a reflection of emotions, thoughts and memories that struck you. Which ones were the hardest to answer? What, if any, experience(s) did you forget until you read a question that caused you to remember? What questions do you still have about yourself? Others?

Questions:

a. Are you an only child?
b. Were you adopted?
c. Have you ever been to Disney World or Disneyland?
d. Have you ever worn braces? (This can be braces on your teeth, hands, wrists, legs.)
e. Have you ever visited another country?
f. Were you ever suspended in middle school? High school?
g. Did you ever fall asleep during school while in a class?
h. Did you ever cut a class? And, if you did, did you get caught?

i. Do you care what others think about you?

j. Do you have a parent(s) who did not graduate from high school?

k. Do you have two mothers or two fathers?

l. Growing up, were you ever bullied?

m. Growing up, did you ever bully others?

n. Have you ever tried something that scared you?

o. Do you judge other people?

p. Have you ever been wrongly judged by others?

q. Did you live with only one parent growing up?

r. Do you believe in love at first sight?

s. Have you ever questioned your religion?

t. Do you know someone who is racist?

u. Do you know where you can buy illegal drugs?

v. Do you know someone who has used illegal drugs?

w. Do you know someone who is suffering from an addiction?

x. Do you have anyone in your family, or close friend, who is an alcoholic?

y. Have you ever lied to a parent? Friend? Spouse? Lover? Boss? Coworker? Teacher?

z. Do you prefer being by yourself?

1. Have you ever been the subject of gossip?

2. Have you ever been unable to afford to buy food or clothes?

3. Have you ever had your gas, electricity or water turned off because you could not pay the bill(s)?

4. Have you ever been homeless?

5. Have you ever been asked to join a gang?

6. Do you know someone who is in a gang?

7. Do you know someone who has been raped?

8. Do you know someone who has been sexually assaulted?

9. Do you know someone who has been killed in a car accident?

10. Do you know someone who is fighting a life-threatening disease?

11. Do you know someone who has died from cancer?

12. Do you know someone who has been a victim of abuse?

13. Have you ever lost a close friend or family member to violence?

14. Do you have a family member who has or is doing time in jail?

15. Are you scared as to what your future holds for you?

16. Do you feel you have ever disappointed someone? Yourself?

17. Do you have a close friend or family member who has committed suicide?

18. Have you ever been teased because of your height/weight or the way you walk or talk?

19. Have you ever been teased or threatened because of the color of your skin?

20. Do you have someone in your family who is transgender? Gay? Bisexual?

21. Have you ever lived with violence?

22. Have you ever heard gunshots?

23. Have you ever been scared in your neighborhood or home currently or in the past?

Answering the Question you are Trying to Ignore

Exercise #17- Silent Reflection

"Reflection: Looking back so that the view looking forward is even clearer."
Unknown

Step One: Sit silently for twenty minutes; no music, conversation, reading or writing. Take inventory of the feelings in your heart. Consider why these feelings are coming up.

Step Two: After twenty minutes, write what needs to be written.

"Self-reflection is a humbling process. It is essential to find out why you think, say and do certain things... then, better yourself."
Sonya Teclai

Self-Reflection

Exercise #18- The Things You Carry

"We all carry these things inside that no one else can see. They hold us down like anchors, they drown us out at sea."
Chelsea Smile

Teaching *The Things They Carried*, by Tim O'Brien, is a riveting favorite of Anne's. It makes you question what is real and what is fiction, and it makes for an excellent writing prompt! What do you carry?

Step One: Read the excerpt below from Tim O'Brien's, *The Things They Carried*, a novel about fighting in the Vietnam War.

The things they carried were largely determined by necessity. Among the necessities or near-necessities were P-38 can openers, pocket knives, heat tabs, wristwatches, dog tags, mosquito repellent, chewing gum, candy, cigarettes, salt tablets, packets of Kool-Aid, lighters, matches, sewing kits, Military Payment Certificates, C rations, and two or three canteens of water. Together, these items weighed between 15 and 20 pounds, depending on a man's habits or rate of metabolism. Henry Dobbins, who was a big man, carried extra rations; he was especially fond of canned peaches in heavy syrup over pound cake. Dave Jensen, who practiced field hygiene, carried a toothbrush, dental floss, and several hotel-sized bars of soap he'd stolen on R&R in Sydney.

(...) They carried all the emotional baggage of men who might die. Grief, terror, love, longing – these were intangibles, but the intangibles had their own mass and specific gravity, they had tangible weight. They carried shameful memories. They carried the common secret of cowardice barely restrained, the instinct to run or freeze or hide, and in many respects this was the heaviest burden of all, for it could never be put down, it required perfect balance and perfect posture.

Step Two: Each of us carries things with us every day, some we can see and some we cannot see. Make a list of all the tangible items you carry with you, the things you *can* see. Examples include: car keys, house keys, lipstick, wallet, credit cards, and my mother's ring. Possibly also state how much each item weighs.

Step Three: Create a list of intangible things you carry. These are the things others *cannot* see. Examples can include: sadness, burdens, sickness, and loneliness. Again, think about how much each thing weighs and why.

Step Four: Read over your list and pick two or three things you carry, being sure to include at least one item from each list.

Step Five: Begin writing using the following questions as your guide: Why did you choose each item? Do any of them hold special significance to you? What item(s) wears you down? What can you get rid of and what do you choose to hold on to? What do you carry and what carries you?

"I know that sometimes the things we carry become too much for us. We are burned down, but somehow we have to pick ourselves up and keep going."
Paulina Simons

Tangible/Intangible

The Things You Carry

Exercise #19- Death

*"The fear of death follows from the fear of life.
A man who lives fully is prepared to die at any time."*
Mark Twain

Death is a part of life, and your thoughts on death majorly affect the way you live your life. We all remember the first feeling of losing something or someone and realizing nothing will ever bring them back. Anne's first experience with death was her grandmother when she died a few months before she was to be married. However, her mother's death had the deepest effect on her.

She was my hero and my best friend. She battled a rare form of cancer and fought valiantly for over three years. During her battle, I would accompany her to chemotherapy, spend days and nights just talking with her and cherishing each moment I was blessed to have. On a warm September morning, she lost the fight. She had been in a "coma-like" state for a few days and, when she took her last breath, a beautiful white dove carried her away. Watching her pass peacefully left me with a sense of comfort and love, helping to ease the pain that still lives in the deepest part of my heart and soul.

That is one, personal experience of death. What is yours? Maybe it was in the loss of a parent, a close friend, or a loving pet. Dealing with a loss can be hard to explain and even harder to describe on paper. However, by doing so, you can learn much about yourself.

Step One: On the following pages, you will find poems written by Donna S. As you read, look for words or phrases that connect to your own experiences.

Step Two: Write what you know needs to be written. Listen to what your heart is trying to tell you. If this is difficult, pretend you are talking with a friend as you write, play your loved one's favorite song or watch their favorite TV program. Once you start, let your emotions bleed through your pen...

*"How can the dead be truly dead when they still live
in the souls of those who are left behind?"*
Carson McCullers

Too Young, by Donna S.

No truth lends light
To why

Or how to say
Good-bye

Your breath has stopped
Today

Tears form and slide
Away

Blue sky, white clouds
And you

Float high, span wide
It's true

His Sister's Home, by Donna S.

Ten wooden bookshelves
waiting to be filled.
Boxes of books in
every room,
creating energy and purpose
in this new space.

Thoreau, Hemingway, Matisse—
Reference goes here, he said.
Art on top.

He was very precise,
my uncle was, about the order.
Here was control;
here was meaning.
Life represented in
loved words, textures,
smells, spines.

Even as the symbols blurred,
brain cells under pressure,
eyes squinting through
soft lamp light,
the words shaky—

Did they all fit?
he asked.

Greta at the funeral, by Donna S.

There was much to take in,
and she was quiet,
offering a shy smile and the simple
word hello, when spoken to.

Sixteen years old,
seeing cousins once removed,
second cousins,
great aunts and uncles,
many for the first time.
Slightly overwhelming,
perhaps,
the familiar looking strangers,
but it was the beauty she noticed.

A slide show was shown,
pictures from her grandmother's childhood—
pony rides,
teenagers posed by large,
antique-looking cars,
a suitor with an Elvis haircut.
A close-up of her grandmother and a sister
with wide, full smiles,
white, even teeth,
sparkling eyes full of laughter
and mischief (or simply joy?)
shining with intelligence.
Curly hair,
strong brows
high cheekbones,
framed kind, kindred faces.

I didn't know Grandma's family
looked like that, she said.
Grandma was so beautiful.
Everyone…
is so beautiful.

Dealing with Loss

Exercise #20- Quote Reflection

"Life is only a reflection of what we allow ourselves to see."
Unknown

While putting this workbook together, a young man offered his thoughts on writing, which are below. Sometimes, less is more. Sometimes, the simplest words are the most profound.

Step One: Read, then read again, the quote below.

Step Two: Answer the following question(s):

- When do love, anger, fear and hate feel like the same emotion?
- Have you ever experienced all of these emotions at once?
- Is one emotion stronger than another?
- What emotion do you strongly connect with?

To me, writing is everything.
It is my anger, it is my fear,
it is my sadness and most importantly,
it is my happiness.
One paper can be filled with pain
and with love all at once.
It is the perfect blend.
It is my escape.
Felix B.

"I am a reflection of my own soul."
Unknown

Emotions

Exercise #21- Once Upon a Time

"Once upon a time something happened, and it was better than something not happening. The End."
Dan Harmon

Growing up, hearing the words, "Once upon a time...", allowed us to dream of faraway lands and handsome princes waiting to whisk us away to colorful lands that existed only in fairy tales. So many memories that cause us to miss the simpler days...

This writing exercise is meant to challenge you in a different way than previously experienced. Bring with you your imagination and do not be afraid to let the words take you away to a land where fairy tales exist...

Step One: Choose a fairy tale – any tale at all. Ideas include *Cinderella, Sleeping Beauty, The Gingerbread Man, The Princess and the Pea, Jack and the Beanstalk*. The list is endless!

Step Two: Enter the story by shifting the point of view so that you are writing in the first person. For example, if you choose the fairy tale *Cinderella*, you may write: Once upon a time, when I was a married, young mother of three, my mom died and my heart broke. A few years later, my dad remarried, etc. Or, write in third person. For example, Once upon a time a young mother of three lost her best friend, her mother. Her heart was never the same.

Step Three: Include as many of the original details of the story as you like, or alter the details as needed. The fairy tale you choose is at the core of your writing, but you can shift perspective and take it wherever you wish. Simply begin at the beginning with *Once upon a time....*

Step Four: When you have finished your story, reflect on what you wrote. Was this exercise easy? Difficult? Why or why not? What emotions did this writing reveal? What did you learn about yourself?

"Fairy tales are more than true: not because they tell us that dragons exist, but because they tell us that dragons can be beaten."
G.K. Chesterton

Once Upon a Time

Exercise #22- Musical Interlude

As was done in the first section of Writing Through the Mess, it is time for you to take a step back from your writing, relax and listen. Listen to your heart. Listen to what your inner muse is trying to say. Listen to the quiet that is trying to escape. Take this time to simply listen. Below are the words to *A Dream is a Wish*, written by Al Hoffman, Jerry Livingston and Mack David, one of the iconic Disney musical masterpieces. Listen to this song if you wish, or pick your own song, or sit in complete silence, if you wish. What is important is to breathe, relax and listen with no interruptions.

Step One: Find a quiet place and take your journal/book with you.

Step Two: Sit quietly and, if you choose, play your favorite music.

Step Three: Listen.

Step Four: Write as much or as little as you need to at this particular moment.

A Dream is a Wish...

A dream is a wish your heart makes
When you're fast asleep
In dreams you will lose your heartache
Whatever you wish for you keep

Have faith in your dreams and someday
Your rainbow will come smiling through
No matter how your heart is grieving
If you keep on believing

The dream that you wish will come true
A dream is a wish your heart makes
When you're feeling small
Alone in the night you whisper

Thinking no one can hear you at all
You wake with the morning sunlight
To find fortune that is smiling on you

Don't let your heart be filled with sorrow
For all you know tomorrow
The dream that you wish will come true

When you can dream then you can start
A dream is a wish you make with your heart

When you can dream then you can start
A dream is a wish you make with your heart

A dream is a wish your heart makes
When you're fast asleep
In dreams you will lose your heartache
Whatever you wish for you keep

You wake with the morning sunlight
To find fortune that is smiling on you
Don't let your heart be filled with sorrow
For all you know tomorrow

The dream that you wish will come true
No matter how your heart is grieving
If you keep on believing
The dream that you wish will come true

When you can dream then you can start
A dream is a wish you make with your heart
When you can dream then you can start
A dream is a wish you make with your heart

When you can dream then you can start
A dream is a wish you make with your heart

What Are You Afraid to Dream

Exercise #23- Putting Your Soul on Paper

"Put your ear down close to your soul and listen and listen hard."
Anne Sexton

Our souls have much to say, if only we stop and listen. Sometimes the pain we are experiencing and the hurt we are feeling have no way to escape. Writing can become the release that frees our soul and, in turn, can possibly save another.

Step One: Read the poem, song and reflection written by Johnston K.

Step Three: What thoughts and/or images come to mind? What words were you drawn to as you read the poem and song? What struggles have you encountered and how did you overcome them? Do you have a poem or song that saved your life? Do you have a piece of writing you have kept? Why did you keep it? Who wrote it? Write what is in your soul as you listen to it.

"Her soul was too deep to explore by those who only swam in the shallow end."
AJ Lawless

POEM
Johnston K.

I strive for simplicity,
But my mind has a knack for complicating things,
It seems, I'm driftwood amongst a wreckage,

I was once crafted by a master artisan and placed carefully
amongst my sanded and stained colleagues, But leagues of harsh
winds and strong waves took their toll,

I now drift aimlessly through the world of the unknown,
And it is shown, quite honestly by my appearance I have grown,
but also faded,
I've become jaded, the thing I use to loved, are now things I have
hated,

Berated by myself and others,
Sometimes the strongest winds come from within your own head,
Some winds will motivate you,
Some will destroy you instead,

Thought to be dead, was the sense of control I was fed,
By the sailors who pull on the ropes,
But they are mistaken by dread,
But I learned that although the wind directs,
The sail has always led,
And in that same respect,
You can't control the winds in your mind,
But you adjust your sail toward the homestead,

We cannot control life,
That is naive,
We can only adjust how we live it,
And rethink the things that we see

SONG
Johnston K.

Came over to my house, sometime after the fight
I tried to hide the crying but a tear caught the light,
You held me all night, you didn't make a sound,
(Until you said)
No matter how shitty life gets, you can turn it around,

Her boyfriend started to beat her, she knew she needed help,
He said if you leave me, I'll go and kill myself,
She needed an escape, well she's got pills for that now,
But I still somehow think, that she can turn it around,

Got a friend who chases demons, with a shot of jack,
Sees dead friends in his nightmares, and their brand new epitaphs,
Between tears, he slams his ninth shot that night down,
Though he thinks me naive, I think he'll turn it around

When you love somebody and it's not the love you thought you found
When the ones that you call friends have really, let you down
Through all the pain in life, there's small truths I have found,
No matter how shitty life gets, you can turn it around

Yeah you can turn it around,
Oh won't you turn it around,
Please god turn this around

I was still in college when I wrote this song. I was struggling mentally. There were several external factors in my life that led me into a deep depression. My best friend that I made while I was at college, just got back from a mental hospital after an intense depressive episode in which he was seriously contemplating suicide. He was crashing on my couch, because he found out the girl whom he was living with and had been dating for the last two years had cheated on him. This situation and drugs, no doubt contributed to the suicidal thoughts.

While he was living on my couch, I would be awoken almost every night by him drunkenly crying, and almost every night I would talk him down from suicidal thoughts.

He came from a run-down former steel town called Easton, PA. There was currently a wave of heroin crashing through his hometown. As the months rolled by, he watched more and more "RIP" Facebook statuses because another hometown friend overdosed on heroin. He even witnessed one of his friends overdose and die right in front of him. As a result, he developed both post-traumatic stress disorder and major depressive disorder. On one of those drunken, depressed nights, he told me he sees his dead friends' faces when he sleeps and that he drinks every night in the hopes that he won't dream and just pass out. Seeing him go through all that pain made me feel useless.

Just that week, I had also found out that my good friend's four-year relationship had become abusive. He started to hit her hard enough to cause bruising and saying things like "If you leave me, I'll kill myself".

Our friends all got together to try and get her to break up with her d*** bag of a boyfriend, but unfortunately, it was not as successful as we hoped. A couple days later, I found out that she got herself a prescription of Xanax to deal with the stress of this relationship. I even heard her jokingly say "a pill a day, keeps the pain at bay".

On top of all these things happening, I was struggling with my own depression, which was more existential in nature. My depression was filled with loneliness, apathy towards life, and a strong focus on inadequacies, fueled by my physical issues. (sciatica, back muscle pain, and digestive issues).

All this blended into a perfect shit stew, a brewing rumination inside my own head. I needed a way to get all this weight off my chest. I needed to change something. A large part of me felt so out of control.

First I wrote the poem, which was a more symbolic outlet for me to express how I was feeling at the moment. A couple days after writing the poem it was if there was an itch that still needed to be scratched. I needed to do something more for my friends than this stupid poem. I was thinking about what to do while playing guitar. I needed to tell those two friends how I felt, but how? I was so utterly scared of confronting them in person. I was playing guitar while thinking of a way to talk to them about it and I struck a couple notes that sounded good and thought "duh! this is totally how I'm going to do it!". The two friends mentioned previously were always big supporters of me musically. So, I wrote the song.

The song came out extremely literal, rather than symbolic and I was scared to play it for them. Things are a lot easy to think about saying then they are to actually say. Eventually, I nervously read the poem and played the song for them and to my surprise, they loved it.

Writing that poem and song not only helped me deal with my problems and the weight put on me by my friend's problems, but it also helped my friends realize their situations were a lot worse when viewed from an outside perspective.

My friend who had suicidal thoughts is now in Alcoholics Anonymous and Narcotics Anonymous and is a little bit more than a month sober. The girl with the abusive boyfriend is now broken up with him and he did not kill himself. She moved out of the apartment they shared. As a result, she has stopped taking pills.

Both friends said that the song and poem helped them think about things in a different light and let them know how much their situations were affecting me. This goes to show that poetry and music can be therapeutic for both the writer and the listener. My advice to any writer would be 1. To never stop and never give up and 2. Don't pull your punches because the most beautiful writing is when somebody puts their soul on to paper.

Johnston K.

Exercise #24- How to Be Ms. Sader

I remember my first-grade teacher. She was a nun. She used to pick her nose, then her ear and then eat it! At least, that is what my first-grade self remembers. She was also my babysitter when my parents went on vacation without us. She caught me smoking cigarettes in second grade and never told on me. So, in hindsight, I guess my second-grade self would say she was just "okay." Today, as a former teacher, she was a person who emulated strict discipline but was a secret teddy bear. She was the perfect combination of opposites. She was Sister Rosalie.

Some of our best writing can come from the ideas of others. *How to Be Mrs. Sader*, written by Vicki Spandel, is one such piece. Through this small poem, the reader learns much about the writer by delving into the quirks, nuances and musings which make a person whole. What makes you who you are?

Step One: Read over the poem, *How to Be Ms. Sader*, written by Vickie Spandel. Also, read the poem Anne wrote about Sister Rosalie. While she could never be her, it was fun trying!

Step Two: Create your own poem using the title, How to Be _. Think about your quirks and all the things which make you unique. What do you think others would say your quirky habits are? Be sure to write this poem about YOU. (You can try writing about someone else another time - that can be interesting, too). Have fun writing!

How to Be Ms. Sader
Vicki Spandel

Avoid giving compliments.
Keep all treats to yourself.
Wear BIG shoes.
Use your voice as a weapon.
Train your face not to smile.
Learn to smell young children coming.
Use industrial strength soap.
Flare your nostrils as you speak.
Make good posture your mission.
Assign more homework than the parents can finish.
Never blink.
Never apologize.

How to Be Sr. Rosalie
Anne Schober

Wear dark clothes with a giant cross hanging from your neck.
Be strict.
Be very strict.
Eat things that make your students say "EW".
Pretend to be nice on Parent/Teacher nights.
Never smile.
Hide a teddy bear heart within a tough exterior.
Be a teacher others strive to be.
Love unconditionally.
Be someone that others remember long after they are gone.

How to Be...

Exercise #25- My Mother Always Wanted

"If you live for people's acceptance, you will die from their rejection."
Lecrae

I was born with my legs turned all-kinds-of-ways, and lived the first two years of my life in leg braces. My parents told me that I was constantly smiling and they never allowed me to feel like I was different or handicapped. As I grew, my feet remained flat and my knees buckled in, but I walked with a determination of fortitude and strength. Until I went to school. I was made fun of for walking differently and I had to have "cookies" put in my shoes to help me with my painful feet. My older sister started ballet and I knew I wanted to do the same. For the first few years, I was quite the dancer. It hurt to point my toes, but I never complained. Until it came time for toe shoes. I tried on a pair and realized I would never be able to dance again. I hung up my ballet shoes and took up kick ball in its place and loved every moment. Through it all, my parents allowed me to discover myself through my unique talents. They never pushed me to do something I did not want to do. They let me be me.

I am lucky. There are many who struggle with living up to parents' wishes and dreams. Sometimes feeling that they can never please them, no matter how hard they try. This exercise is meant for you to examine your relationship with your parents and, in turn, enlighten you as to who you are, where you come from, and who you strive to be.

Step One: Read the poem, "My Mother Always Wanted," by Heejung K. Begin by writing the words "My mother always wanted…", or "My parents always wanted…", or "My father always wanted…". You can use anyone you wish to make this writing your own.

Step Two: Continue writing. Perhaps borrow a line or word from the poem if you feel stuck. But write as much as you can using details to enhance your thoughts.

Step Three: When you have finished, reflect on what you wrote. What memories did you recall? What images sprang forth from your mind onto the paper? Are you still trying to please someone? Why?

"Trying to live up to everyone's expectations is like trying to cup the ocean in your hands. Impossible much?"
Unknown

My Mother Always Wanted
By Heejung K

My mother always wanted
a graceful daughter
so she enrolled me in
Madam Dupont's School of Ballet
for young Mademoiselles.
I practiced for a month
until my toes
bled and my legs throbbed.
I quit, gracefully.
Then my mother hired
a tutor, so that I
could excel in my studies.
I didn't like this
woman and eventually
told her "You have a
bad attitude."
She never came back.
I grinned, excellently.
My mother then convinced
me to take violin lessons. At first
I loved the responsibility
and the sophistication needed to play
such a sleek instrument,
which cost my parents
a hefty sum. But the
sticky rosin, the
laborious practicing, and
the heavy case thudding
against my leg
became tiresome.
I packed the violin away, quietly.
When will she learn?

My _____ Always Wanted

Exercise #26- Revisiting Your Writing

**"You don't write because you want to say something.
You write because you have something to say."
F. Scott Fitzgerald**

A lot of soul searching happened in this section. Many questions were asked of you and some were, no doubt, hard to answer. Digging deep means finding what lies beneath. Before moving on to the next section, take the time and revisit what you have written. Maybe there is a question you need to explore further. Maybe you left a writing piece half-written and you want to finish. Maybe you wrote something so powerful that you need to go back and re-read your entry. Maybe you just need to reflect on what you have written, where you have been and where you are going. It is important to revisit. It is important to pause. It is important to reflect.

Step One: Revisit your pages of writing, reading and writing as you go.

Step Two: Add to your writing, if necessary. Take a "golden line" from one of your writing pieces, lift it, and begin a new piece. Write questions that you may want to explore more deeply. Whatever you need to do, do it. Be sure to revisit each of your pieces and look deeply into your words by exploring who you are.

**"Write what disturbs you, what you fear, what you have not
been willing to speak about. Be willing to be split open."
Natalie Goldberg**

Split Open a Golden Line

EMBRACING

"Often, it's not about becoming a new person, but becoming the person you were meant to be, and already are, but don't know how to be."

Heath L. Buckmaster

Exercise #27- Forgive Yourself

"There is no sense in punishing your future for the mistakes of your past. Forgive yourself, grow from it, and then let it go."
Melainie Koulouris

I doubt if any of us can say we do not have a single regret. It is hard to forgive ourselves for something we did or said. It does not matter if it happened yesterday, last month, two years ago or even twenty years ago. We are hard on ourselves. But we cannot continue to let these regrets pile up. We need to learn to let go. We need to learn to forgive ourselves. We are not perfect…! It is important to remember that we are doing the best we can at any given point in our lives.

When I look back at my high school and college years, I cringe. I drank too much, stole too much, lied too much and so much more. I was a young person trying to find my way in the world. I was searching for my dreams and for that, I have no regrets. It has taken me a long time to get to this point; writing helped me to unpack all the mixed emotions I had been holding on to for all those many years.

Step One: Read the quote from Maya Angelou, which follows on the next page.

Step Two: Use the following prompts to guide you through this exercise. You can also steal a line from Maya Angelou.

• What are some of your regrets, mistakes, missed opportunities? What do you need to forgive yourself for?

• How is not forgiving yourself serving you? How might you feel different if you forgive yourself for mistakes you have made?

• Write a letter to your younger self offering guidance, compassion and gentleness.

"Take a walk through the garden of forgiveness and pick a flower of forgiveness for everything you have ever done. When you get to that time that is now, make a full and total forgiveness of your entire life and smile at the bouquet in your hands because it truly is beautiful."
Stephen Richards

"I don't know if I continue, even today, always liking myself. But what I learned to do many years ago was to forgive myself. It is very important for every human being to forgive herself or himself because if you live, you will make mistakes- it is inevitable. But once you do and you see the mistake, then you forgive yourself and say, 'Well, if I'd known better I'd have done better,' that's all. So you say to people who you think you may have injured, 'I'm sorry,' and then you say to yourself, 'I'm sorry.' If we all hold on to the mistake, we can't see our own glory in the mirror because we have the mistake between our faces and the mirror; we can't see what we're capable of being. You can ask forgiveness of others, but in the end the real forgiveness is in one's own self. I think that young men and women are so caught by the way they see themselves. Now, mind you, when a larger society sees them as unattractive, as threats, as too black or too white or too poor or too fat or too thin or too sexual or too asexual, that's rough. But you can overcome that. The real difficulty is to overcome how you think about yourself. If we don't have that we never grow, we never learn, and sure as hell we should never teach."

Maya Angelou

Forgiving Myself

Exercise #28- Writing a Letter You Would Never Send

"Nights in white satin, never reaching the end.
Letters I've written, never meaning to send."
Mario Frangoulis

"The unsent letter is a form of <u>writing therapy</u> that encourages you to address a letter to someone you don't feel you can talk directly to – perhaps a former lover, a friend you've fallen out with, or perhaps someone who has died. It's a way of putting into words a deeply held thought or feeling that has somehow been damaging you in some way, or holding you back. The idea is that you write about your feelings openly – so they're 'out there' – but you don't have to send the letter. The point is to articulate and process your feelings rather than openly hurt someone else by sending the letter." (<u>www.worthwrite.wordpress.com</u>)

Writing a letter you would never send is one of the most therapeutic writing pieces you can create. Maybe you want to admit the truth about something, but you cannot say it openly to whomever you need to. Maybe you need to explore your own feeling about something. Maybe you are angry at someone and you need to get the harsh feelings off your chest. Maybe you need to write to someone who has passed away, saying what you wish you had said while they were alive. Maybe you need to write to your ex-spouse or ex-friend. Maybe you need to write a letter that no one will read until you have passed. Whatever the reason or circumstance, writing a letter you will never send is powerful.

Step One: Write! Write! Write! And, don't forget to breathe. You can start the letter with "Dear _____", or "Hey, Asshole." As you write, you may discover some hidden truths. You may start to re-think and re-evaluate your previous ideas, thoughts, and emotions. You may start finding confidence in what you're feeling. By the end, you will hopefully feel peaceful and more content.

Step Two: Rip up the letter, if you wish, or keep it neatly tucked away in your journal. It is your writing. Your thoughts. Your feelings. Do what you know needs to be done.

"Two words. Three vowels. Four consonants. Seven letters. It can either cut you open to the core and leave you in ungodly pain or it can free your soul and lift a tremendous weight off your shoulders. The phrase is: It's over."
Maggi Richard

I'll Write It, But I Won't Send It!

Exercise #29- Writing a Love Letter to Yourself

"To say "I love you" one must first know how to say the 'I'."
Ayn Rand

A love letter is defined as *a letter or note written by someone to his or her sweetheart or lover.* My husband wrote me a love letter when were engaged and, thirty-three years later, I still have it. It was the most pure, raw and loving letter I have ever received. It made me feel loved, special and protected. But, if we do not love ourselves, can we really accept a love letter written to us? Can we accept the words?

Accepting who we are and loving ourselves is one of the hardest things we can do. And it is time to begin. It is time to embrace ourselves, all of our imperfections, all of our flaws and love who we are and who we will become.

Step One: Begin this exercise with an open heart. There is so much to love about yourself and it is time you start. TODAY.

Step Two: Below are some ideas you can use as you write your own love letter to yourself. Use one, three or all. They are here to help you jumpstart your love letter journey.

1. Begin with "Dear Sexy", "Dear Beautiful", "Dear BFF", "Dear Me"…

2. Tell yourself in the letter why you are writing—how you want yourself to feel. "I'm writing because you deserve to know how much you mean to me," or "I want you to feel in love with yourself by the end of this letter.".

3. In your letter, talk about one thing that is beautiful—your legs, your smile, your eyes. If you can't think of anything, stare into your eyes in front of the mirror with the intention of describing them in detail. Notice flecks of color in your irises, or the way the light plays on your eyes, or how deep you look.

4. Talk about at least one funny thing about you. Things you have said, things you have done, jokes you have told, practical jokes you have played on others - let yourself smile as you remember.

5. Write about the small things you appreciate about yourself. These can include going for walks every morning, going to the gym, drinking smoothies, any little thing. Be sure to say "Thank You" to yourself as you write.

6. Write promises to yourself in your letter.

7. Write a wish you have for yourself. This is can be for today, tomorrow or years from now.

8. And, if you do not know how to start your letter, perhaps try this:

I have the most incredible_____.
When I walk into a room people feel_____ .
It's very easy for me to _____
because I'm so _____. I
will continue to kick ass at _____
because I can't stop being _____   _____.
(uncustomary.org)

9. If you want, put your letter in an envelope, address it to yourself, mail it and wait with bated breath for the mailman to deliver your love letter to yourself!

"You yourself, as much as anybody in the entire universe, deserve your love and affection."
Sharon Salzberg

Dear Me

Exercise #30- A Gratitude Journal

"Give thanks for a little and you will find a lot."
Hausa Proverb

The most difficult time in my life up to this point was when my husband left. He decided he couldn't handle the responsibilities of being a husband and father. For over a year I struggled with handling work and kids and bills and a lawyer and my emotions. I searched for help to heal and found it through Beginning Experience. It was there that I first understood the healing powers of writing.

It's a retreat type weekend I found through my church. I took the plunge and signed up. It was the most powerful weekend of my life, a real turning point in my journey. Speakers shared deeply personal talks on topics associated with divorce. Then we were sent on our own to write and reflect about the topic. It took me half the weekend to allow myself to really open up in my writing and face some difficult things. After each writing session, we met in small groups and could share. At first, I wasn't brave enough to share much. But by Sat. evening, after writing about realistic and unrealistic guilt I really had a breakthrough.

I was later invited to join the team and present for others at BE weekends. In preparing talks to give, I really had to delve deep. We had critiquing sessions to help improve our talks. Talk about feeling vulnerable! But it really taught me that writing can heal. I will forever be grateful for that opportunity.

Around the same time, I saw Oprah discuss gratitude journals on her show. I started one to help keep me from being bogged down by the exhausting moments of everyday. I remember several days when I wrote "It is sunny." or "My boys said I love you to me." It wasn't anything fancy, but it helped me reflect daily on some positives instead of feeling like I was under a black cloud.
Peg M.

Peg found solace in creating a gratitude journal to help her see the good in life when all else seemed to be spiraling out of control. She started focusing on the little things that brought joy to her life instead of the "exhausting moments of everyday". Creating a gratitude journal can help you to see the everyday joys instead of focusing on overwhelming pain, heartache or sadness that often enter our lives.

Louise Jensen wrote the following tips for creating a powerful gratitude journal:

1. Don't just go through the motions. Decide to be consciously more grateful. Feel what you write and believe it.

2. Don't set yourself a minimum number of things to write per day.

Be flexible and don't take the joy away by being too regimented.

3. Don't wait for the right time. Write when you need to ensure you don't forget anything.

4. Elaborating on why you are grateful allows you to really explore your feelings.

5. Focus on people rather than things.

6. Don't rush; savor every word.

7. Include surprises.

8. Keep the negative out.

9. Mix it up. Don't put the same thing every day. Expand your awareness.

10. Be creative. Include photos, tickets to concerts, lists, restaurant receipts, etc.

11. Give it a fair chance. Don't give up or dismiss it as not working.

Let's give it a try!

Step One: You can start your gratitude Journal within the workbook and see how you like it. Then, if you feel inclined, use a separate journal to continue your journey.

Step Two: Find a good time of your day where you can devote a few minutes reflecting on what you are grateful for. It can be as simple as the sun is shining today to a moment that touched your heart in a special way.

Step Three: Try to write consistently in your gratitude for at least 21 days so that you begin to form a habit. Do not give up on it! Focus on the positives!

Step Four: Have fun; and cheers to you for finding happiness in each of your days!

"Live simply. Dream big. Be grateful. Give love. Laugh lots."
Paulo Coehlo

With Gratitude

Exercise #31- Silent Reflection

"*Silence is a true friend who never betrays.*"
Confucious

Step One: Sit silently for twenty minutes; no music, conversation, reading or writing. Take inventory of the feelings in your heart. Consider why these feelings are coming up.

Step Two: After twenty minutes, write what needs to be written.

"*Silence is a source of great strength.*"
LaoTzu

The Strength of Silence

Exercise #32- Questions to Embrace

"We make our world significant by the courage of our questions and by the depth of our answers."
Carl Sagan

Have you ever noticed that your biggest "aha" moments come from someone asking a <u>powerful question</u>? Suddenly everything seems to make a little more sense, and you know what you need to do from that point forward. Asking yourself questions can help you to understand yourself on a deeper, more profound level. By doing so, you embrace who you are completely.

Directions: Read the list of questions that follow and answer the ones that speak to you. Maybe you will feel ready to jump into one question right away or sit and ponder another question for a few minutes, hours or days. This is your journey. Explore your answers. At your own pace.

Questions:

Are your "shoulds" getting in the way of your happiness?

If you achieved all your life's goals, how would you feel? How can you feel that along the way?

What did I learn today?

Who did I love?

What made me laugh?

What would happen if…?

What/Who did you make better today?

What can you do today to improve? Which is worse — failing or ne er trying?

Do you find yourself influencing your world, or it influencing you?

We are always making choices. Are you choosing for your story or for someone else's?

When it's all said and done, will you have *said* more than you've *done*?

What else?

"The question isn't who is going to let me; it's who is going to stop me."
Ayn Rand

"Aha!"

Exercise #33- Vision Board

"Your vision will become clear only when you can look into your own heart. Who looks outside, dreams; who looks inside, awakes."
Carl Jung

A few years ago, I made a vision board. It was filled with images, quotes and dreams. I did not know the power of this simple exercise until I slowly began to see my vision come to life. Trip to Mexico – *Check*. Writing a book – *Check*. Being on the Ellen DeGeneres Show – *Half Check* (that is a story for another book!). Seeing the board daily helped me to visualize my dreams and goals and helped to motivate me into making them a reality.

What is a vision board? It is a visualization tool that you can use as inspiration for your life journey. It is a collection of images, pictures and affirmations of your dreams, goals and all things that make you happy.

How do you make a vision board? Any way you please. There are no rules and you cannot mess it up. Your vision is yours and is meant to remind you of your passions and purpose.

Before creating your own vision board, reflect on the following questions:

- What are your goals? (relationships, career, finances, home, travel, personal growth)
- In your opinion, what is a good life?
- What activities do you want to learn how to do?
- How do you want to be remembered by others?

Step One: Gather the following items:

- Any kind of board – cork, poster, pin/bulletin board or even a notebook to make it portable!
- Scissors, tape, pins, glue stick
- Fun markers, stickers
- Magazines
- Photos

Step Two: Put together your board. Include quotes, sayings, images of places you want to, people, postcards and the list goes on. Use anything that will inspire you and further your vision. Give yourself **at least** an hour or two to put your board together.

Step Three: Place your board in a prominent place where you can see it every day. This can include your office, bathroom, bedroom, kitchen, living room. Be sure to place it somewhere where you are reminded of your vision and dreams every single day.

"The one thing that you have that nobody else has is you. Your voice, your mind, your story, your vision. So write and draw and build and play and dance and live as only you can."
Neil Gaiman

Vision Board Ideas and Themes

Exercise #34- Quote Reflection

"Knowing yourself is the beginning of all wisdom."
Aristotle

Every so often, a quote can cause you to think and reflect. Sometimes, less is more. Sometimes, the simplest words are the most profound.

Step One: Read, then read again, the quote below.

Step Two: Answer the following question(s):

• How can we learn to see the positive when there are so many negatives surrounding us?

• What does the barn symbolize to you?

• Is your mind open to embracing your best self?

"Barn's burnt down.
Now I can see the moon."
Mizuta Masahide

Seeing the Moon

Exercise #35- If You Really Knew Me

"'Are you okay?'
Always the same question.
'I'm fine.'
Always the same lie."
Unknown

There are a lot of ice breaker questions. What is your favorite book? What is your favorite color? What is the last book you read? Who is your favorite band? The list is endless. However, there is not a question as profound as "If I really knew you, what would I know?" It is a question that can make you pause and is difficult to answer.

It is one thing to know a person's title, accomplishments, successes or "image."

It is entirely different to connect to their humanity, to learn the intimate details about them that you would know if you really knew them. Many people are so afraid of getting vulnerable or, as we say at Challenge Day, "getting real," that they end up settling for superficial relationships and conversations rather than risking the possibility of sharing more personally, and then perhaps being rejected. People often compare their "insides" to other people's "outsides," and relate image-to-image rather than heart- to-heart.

As a result, many of us spend our lives feeling separate and alone.

"Be The Hero You've Been Waiting For," by Yvonne and Rich Dutra-St. John

Knowing who you are is the center of embracing your whole self. Who are you? What would you answer if I saw you on the street and asked, "If I really knew you, what would I know?"

Step One: Answer the following question: *If you really knew me you would know....*

Step Two: Write for as long as you need. Use *"If you really knew me you would know"* as often as you want. Do not be afraid to leave and come back later. Be honest with yourself. Who are you?

"A man is like a novel: until the very last page you don't know how it will end. Otherwise it wouldn't even be worth reading."
Yevgeny Zamyatin

If You Really Knew Me

Exercise #36- Remembering What You Love

"Let the beauty of what you love be what you do."
Rumi

Daily, we are bogged down by the necessary tasks we must accomplish, leaving little time for much else. Whether you are a new mom, a successful business man or a teen maneuvering through the rigors of school and life, we have little time left to do the things we love. When I was teaching, I would spend eight hours a day in the classroom and then another four to five hours at night grading and creating lesson plans. I left little time in my life for what mattered most: myself, my husband, and my family. We would go away on trips and the beautiful scenery passed me by as I had my head down in the piles of papers I brought with me. I had to do something. I was exhausted. I was losing myself in the daily life of being a teacher. And, I did something drastic. I quit. I left my teaching world behind to do what I always dreamed: writing. It was a big jump and the uncertainty caused many sleepless nights, but I knew I had to do something before I lost everything around me. Including myself.

While quitting a job is often not the answer, remembering what we love and making time for it, is. Life is short. Do what you love and love what you do.

Step One: Make a list. What makes you happy? What makes your heart sing? What lights you up?

Step Two: Answer the following questions:

• How often do you do the things on your list?

• Are there some things you were afraid to write down? Why?

• How can you make time for the things on your list?

• If you won the lottery and never had to work again, how would you spend your days?

"The ultimate dream in life is to be able to do what you love
and learn something from it. "
Jennifer Love Hewitt

Learn From What You Love

Exercise #37- Creating a Bucket List

"Don't worry, I plan on living a long time."
"Why are you making a bucket list, then?"
"Because if you wait until you're really dying, it's too late."
Gayle Forman

About ten years ago, I watched the movie *The Bucket List*. Two men, over a course of three months, traveled the world together crossing items off their bucket list. It caused me to pause and think how fragile life is and what I want to do before my time comes. I quickly made a list. Coach one play at the University of Notre Dame. Visit every state. Own a Saint Bernard. Live in a tiny house. Get on stage and sing with Jimmy Buffet. Have an audience with the pope. My list is as eclectic as I am. But it is mine. While it bears some similarities with a Vision Board, a Bucket List is more about experiences you want to have before you die. Life is short. Don't put things off. Don't wait for the perfect circumstances.

Below is a collection of items that others have placed on their Bucket Lists to get your creative juices flowing. The sky is the limit.

1. Go to a drive-in movie
2. Learn to play the banjo
3. Stand on the North or South Pole
4. Visit every continent
5. Dive with sharks
6. Go the moon
7. Go somewhere with zero gravity
8. Go on a Safari
9. Stay in an over-the-water bungalow on a tropical island
10. Be in a flash mob

Step One: Dream! Create your list removing all limitations. Nothing is too outrageous. What do you want to do before you die? What do you plan to do with your one crazy and wild life?

Step Two: Begin planning! Have fun!

"One day your life will flash before your eyes.
Make sure it is worth watching."
The Bucket List

Bucket List

Exercise #38- I Am Enough

"I am strong.
I am beautiful.
I am enough."
Vanessa Pawlowski

We live in a culture with a strong sense of scarcity. "We wake up in the morning and we say, 'I didn't get enough sleep.' And we hit the pillow saying, 'I didn't get enough done.'" We're never thin enough, extraordinary enough or good enough – until we decide that we are. "For me," says Brene Brown, "the opposite of scarcity is not abundance. It's enough. I'm enough. My kids are enough."

I am enough. For many of us, those three words are hard to utter. For a very long time, I faked those words. I would add a "but" or an "if" after those three simple words. Sometimes I still can't say it, and that is okay. But, every day I try to remind myself that I. Am. Enough.

Barry Lane, in his book *The Healing Pen*, asks his readers to do the following:

Find a full-length mirror if you can. Stand in front of it. Look at the story of your life in your face, your eyes and the other parts of your body. Think of all the writing you have done in your journal and the stories yet to be told. See the pain, the joy, the fear, the sadness, the awe of your life on this planet. Look closely into your eyes and know that you are here for a reason.

We are asking you to do the same. Stand in front of a mirror, look deep into your eyes and say to your reflection: **I am enough!** Say it loud, say it proud and say it until you believe it. Do not add any "buts" or "ifs." You are enough! Embrace yourself and all that you are. When you are ready, grab your journal.

Step One: Repeating I Am Enough, begin writing your story. I am enough.

Here is an example:

I am enough. I am quiet, loud, obnoxious and sincere all at the same time. I am imperfect. I am not defined by my weight, but am defined by my curves and beautiful smile. I am unique. I love to watch football, throw back a few beers and mow the grass on a crisp, fall day. I am enough.

Step Two: Continue writing what needs to be written. Remember, YOU ARE ENOUGH!

"No matter how much I get done, or is left UNDONE,
at the end of the day, I am enough."
Brene Brown

I Wish You Enough

I wish you enough sun to keep your attitude bright no matter how grey the day may appear.

I wish you enough rain to appreciate the sun even more.

I wish you enough happiness to keep your spirit alive and everlasting.

I wish you enough pain so that even the smallest of joys in life may appear bigger.

I wish you enough gain to satisfy your wanting.

I wish you enough loss to appreciate all that you possess.

I wish you enough hellos to get you through the final good-bye.

Bob Perkins

I Am Enough

Exercise #39- There is Writing

You have so much left to write. You are nearing the end of the exercises in this book, but there is always writing. You can write at any time. Writing can see you through. Your life, your story, continues. There is still so much to be said. Writing is a powerful tool and there are many words left to discover. Write what needs to be written.

Step One: Read the following story from Tiffany D.

Step Two: Answer the following questions:

1. What do you still need to write?

2. How has writing helped you to heal?

3. Try your own piece where you repeat the phrase, "But there is writing."

Step Three: Never stop writing!

There Is Writing

It was a dark year, a tough year. In only a 365-day span I lost my father and grandmother to cancer, one a long war with a series of vicious battles, while the other was sudden and shocking; I lost my cat of nineteen years, graduated college, quit my job, gained a career, was laid off in a mass 500-person-layoff from said career, and my then-boyfriend (now-husband) and I dealt with a horrendous roommate in court and decidedly shouldered a painful relocation. Six months later I gained four two-month-old cats and dogs and another move to Los Angeles to search for more jobs. It was hectic and wild and filled with so much stress that I shocked doctors at how I'd managed to get through it without being medicated.

But there was writing.

During this time I turned to my novel. My words. My ideas. They kept me company. During the arguments, during the sadness and stress, during the questions and fears. They were there. I finished my first draft of the novel while I searched for new jobs. My boyfriend supported me every step of the way. He thought I could "be" something. A real author.

A mere six months later, my then-boyfriend lost his Los Angeles job and the only opportunity we could find was in Louisiana. We packed our animals, cars, and 26-foot-UHaul and moved with high hopes. A year later, however, that company closed their southern branch and we were forced to move again – to an opportunity in New Jersey. I compartmentalized my stress, only given away by the new patch of silver growing from my roots.

But there was writing.

Our time in Louisiana was an adventure. We became engaged and I self-published a book of poetry. I attended conferences, refined my novel, and queried agents. And I wrote. I dove into the writing. It allowed me to step away from the hectic life we were living. My characters were still there. Their chaotic plot still swirled around them. Every time we packed or unpacked became a pause button on the life of my novel, but it was still there. It waited for me. It became my rock. I could always return to it if I needed an escape. And my fiancé supported me every step of the way. He thought I could "be" something. A real author.

So we packed it all up and moved to New Jersey. Everything seemed fine, the job was great... But another year later our landlord decided to sell the property and forced us out. I stood shell-shocked. It felt like we were running farther away, constantly lost and searching for where we belonged. The deaths in my family never felt properly grieved for. Unable to hold down a job during all this, I became far-removed from the job market and the skills I gained in college. It became unbearable for me to even apply for a job. I lost myself.

I forgot who I was and what I could become. Anxiety, stress, and sadness ruled my life. Self-doubt was a power player and self-deprecation, its tyrannical ruler. I've been in the spiral. It's common for writers to find themselves in it. That whirl of pain and worry and uncertainty.

But there is writing.

Whatever reservations and hesitancies there are, there is writing. It's still there. It's always been there. Whether the writing of the day is terrible or wonderful or nonexistent. It becomes your rock, always waiting for you to chisel away at it. I've had editors, I've met with agents, I've attended conferences. As I polished the rough draft into something salable, I've also polished myself into something stronger. The book is different than when I started. As am I. And my husband supports me every step of the way. He still thinks I can "be" something. A real author.

Perhaps someday.

But either way, no matter what happens, there will be writing.

Tiffany D.

There is Writing

Exercise #40- Song Reflection

Ending with this song is perfect. There is much left for you to write. Your story is not complete. As Natasha says so perfectly… "I am unwritten, can't read my mind, I'm undefined."

Step One: Listen to this beautiful piece of music. Reflect on the words and how it relates to you and where you are at this moment.

Step Two: Write what is still unwritten. Write what is in your heart.

Unwritten
Natasha Bedingfield

I am unwritten, can't read my mind, I'm undefined
I'm just beginning, the pen's in my hand, ending unplanned

Staring at the blank page before you
Open up the dirty window
Let the sun illuminate the words that you could not find

Reaching for something in the distance So close you can almost
taste it Release your inhibitions
Feel the rain on your skin
No one else can feel it for you
Only you can let it in
No one else, no one else
Can speak the words on your lips Drench yourself in words unspoken Live your life with arms wide open Today is where your book begins The rest is still unwritten

Oh, oh, oh

I break tradition, sometimes my tries are outside the lines
We've been conditioned to not make mistakes, but I can't live that
way

Staring at the blank page before you
Open up the dirty window
Let the sun illuminate the words that you could not find

Reaching for something in the distance So close you can almost
taste it Release your inhibitions
Feel the rain on your skin
No one else can feel it for you
Only you can let it in
No one else, no one else

Can speak the words on your lips Drench yourself in words unspoken Live your life with arms wide open Today is where your book
begins

Feel the rain on your skin
No one else can feel it for you
Only you can let it in
No one else, no one else
Can speak the words on your lips Drench yourself in words unspo-
ken Live your life with arms wide open Today is where your book
begins The rest it still unwritten

Staring at the blank page before you
Open up the dirty window
Let the sun illuminate the words you could not find

Reaching for something in the distance So close you can almost
taste it Release your inhibitions
Feel the rain on your skin
No one else can feel it for you
Only you can let it in
No one else, no one else
Can speak the words on your lips Drench yourself in words unspo-
ken Live your life with arms wide open Today is where your book
begins

Feel the rain on your skin
No one else can feel it for you
Only you can let it in
No one else, no one else
Can speak the words on your lips Drench yourself in words unspo-
ken Live your life with arms wide open Today is where your book
begins The rest is still unwritten
The rest is still unwritten
The rest is still unwritten

Write What is Still Unwritten

Thank you for joining us on this journey.
Life is messy.
But it is through the mess that wisdom comes.
We are more likely to find that core of wisdom if we write.
Remember the power of the written word!
It is your word, your life, your wisdom.

Anne and Lisa